THE FIFTH REVOLUTION

Reinventing workplace
happiness, health, and
engagement through
compassion

DR. IMMANUAL JOSEPH, PH.D.

Dear Marc

Thank you for inspiring the world with your wisdom and kindness. You are an inspiration and I am honored to know you!

Best Wishes

DEDICATION

This book is dedicated to all the giants whose shoulders have carried me, for, without them, I would have missed the forest for the trees.

Table of Contents

SECTION 3: COMPASSION EXPERIMENTS   199

SECTION 4: A SYSTEMS APPROACH TO COMPASSION   228

INTRODUCTION

Two Heart Attacks

Melissa Sutor

Mindfulness Teacher and Consultant, Hawaii, USA

"Years ago, I worked as a project manager at a tech startup in Silicon Valley. I was tasked with ensuring that the company's flagship product was delivered on time and within budget. Startups can be challenging places to work in. Expectations were high, and timelines were tight. I was particular that work demands should not compromise the health and happiness of the people I was leading. However, the CEO did not see our health and happiness as priorities. He demanded that we work 6- to 7 days per week at 10- to 12 hours per day. His demands overrode our life balance and self--care. My team was crumbling physically, emotionally, mentally, and spiritually, while I was rendered helpless in effecting positive change. I was even labeled as being a "weak woman" for caring about the well-being of the team. The stress that I experienced at work manifested physically as body pains and insomnia.

I was not the only one suffering.

One of the engineers who reported to me ended up in the hospital with severe high blood pressure. I went to the hospital to check on him. When I saw the condition he was in, I pleaded with him to take some time off work and put his health first. He was kept at the hospital overnight for monitoring. He called the next morning to inform me that he was on his way to work. The CEO had threatened to fire him if he did not come back to work immediately and keep the project on schedule. I was appalled!

My heart went out to my friend who chose to be defined by his work. I reached out to friends and recruiters to help him find another position. But he had no time to even go for interviews. I felt crushed having to work in a culture that placed profits over people. My work was not worth the personal damage it was causing. I gave my resignation and asked my friend to take a leap of faith as well. He refused. He was afraid. He refused to see the bigger picture of his life and what this job was doing to him. There was nothing I could do to convince him otherwise.

So I moved on.

Not too long after, I received a call with the news *that my friend had died of a massive heart attack, alone in his apartment.*

So much suffering, and a life needlessly lost!

All because of a CEO who refused to care for his people, and an employee who was not empowered to make appropriate choices in the face of suffering. **"**

Nishita Bharadwaj
IT Delivery Manager at VMware

"Raj (name changed for privacy) was 37 years old when he passed away. At the time of his passing, he was working as a Senior Application Developer in VMware, Bangalore, India. His wife was a homemaker, and his two children were less than ten years old. He had been an employee of VMware for almost three years at that time.

It was a Sunday evening. Raj was with his family, and he asked for a cup of tea. But by the time his wife came back with tea, he had suffered a massive heart attack. She reached out to one of Raj's colleagues, who immediately took him to a hospital. Sadly, Raj was declared dead upon arrival.

One of the first few people to respond to the tragedy was Raj's IT Site Leader at the time, Chandra Elango. Chandra had made it a priority to learn about all of his team members and their families. So when this happened, Chandra had a clear grasp of the challenges that Raj's wife could be facing.

One of the biggest challenges was navigating the legal framework to allow the release of the body for burial. In the interim, headed by Chandra, we informed HR and initiated a call to action within VMware. VMware is a large organization with offices across the globe. Chandra coordinated a financial response by organizing a global fundraiser to support the family. Raj's wife was not very educated. She was oblivious to the financial arrangements of the household. Because of this, we had to climb through several hoops, talking to banks and regulators to transfer financial ownership to her. To do this, we had to leverage our family and friends heavily. Chandra actively got involved in the response, paying attention to even the smallest details and logistics to support the grieving family. For example, he requested a female colleague to stay in touch with Raj's widow to make sure that there was someone available for sensitive discussions.

Raj's hometown was nearly 110 miles away from Bangalore in a different Indian state. We arranged for Raj's body to be transported to his native village. None of this was easy, as there was no precedence. We were only guided by our genuine care for a colleague who had passed away, and our concern for his family who were in distress. VMWare gave us the flexibility to provide compassionate responses, not stopping with financial support, but also providing the space and culture for those responses to happen. We are lucky to have leadership that does not mind getting their hands dirty when it comes to caring. VMware's policies allow for 40 hours of paid time every year in community outreach and making a social difference in our communities. It also helps that our CEO, Pat Gelsinger, models human caring in business.

In Raj's situation, most of the challenges happened because he had not taken the effort to include his wife in emergency responses. His wife was not privy to his insurance details and bank accounts. We often had to work backward to get her the resources that were due to her. And I was able to tap into my family's contacts in Bangalore to expedite things. Many VMware IT India team members came together to help at various points. We also made sure that our support extended well beyond an immediate knee-jerk response to suffering. We had collected funds for her, but with two young children, we wanted to ensure long-term comfort. Using our collective network once again, we identified a job opportunity for Raj's widow. Chandra also created an educational fund to support the children through their schooling.

One good thing that came out of this experience was that we set up precedence for human responses in the face of incredible suffering in the workplace. When a similar challenge happened in VMWare later, they used our experiences as a compassion framework for intervention. End of the day, we lost a member of our team but built relationships with the others that will last a lifetime.

Raj's death happened almost six years ago, but we still actively look into the wellbeing of our fallen colleague's family. We know that their loss cannot be compensated, but we can certainly minimize the impact of suffering. This is what compassionate workplaces are all about. **"**

Choices

Viktor Frankl was a successful Jewish neurologist and psychiatrist in pre-world war II Germany. After the Nazis invaded his hometown of Vienna in Austria and things became increasingly difficult for the Jewish people, he obtained an immigration visa to America. But not wanting to desert his aging parents, he chose to let that immigration visa pass. It was a painfully fateful decision, because two years later, the Nazis arrested him. He lost his entire family- his father, mother, wife, brother, and his sister-in-law- to the brutality of the Holocaust.

In his book, 'Man's Search for Meaning,' he recounted the extraordinary cruelty and suffering he witnessed and experienced in the two years as a holocaust prisoner. More importantly, his book highlights the human capacity for resilience and compassion, even in the middle of the sea of human suffering.

"Everything can be taken from a man but one thing: the last of the human freedom," he writes in his book, *"—to choose one's attitude in any given set of circumstances, to choose one's own way."*

Melissa's CEO chose to harm. Chandra, Nishita, and the team chose compassion. One caused suffering. Another alleviated suffering.

Our ability to choose makes us human. But in the rat race of living, we often forget that we have power over our choices. In our choices lie our happiness, peace, and strength. But sometimes, we need reminders. Sometimes we need the inspiration and tools to choose compassion over harm. This is what this book offers. The stories and narratives in this book demonstrate that compassionate responses are possible, even under challenging circumstances.

Although compassion is a framework for every aspect of human living, this book focuses on the practice of compassion in the workplace. Work takes up a massive part of our time and our mind space. The time we spend at work is the most energized part of our day, and where we are primed to give our mental and physical best. When we invest so much time and effort into our workplaces, one would expect that we would do everything in our power to make this part of our living a happy, purpose-filled, and empowering experience. More often than not, workplaces are associated with stress and distress. Burdened by social judgment and comparison, work has become a mad scramble to board the 'nowhere train'. Workplaces are filled with a diverse set of individuals, each bringing unique mindsets, expectations, behaviors, and end-goals to the collective experience. When there is no clear cultural narrative to weave these range of personalities into a common functioning unit, negative outcomes are inevitable.

Work can kill!

Karoshi is a Japanese word, which means 'overwork death.' As hard as it is to believe, some of us literally work ourselves to death. A 2013 article from the International Labor Organization identifies some typical cases of Karoshi, including the case of an employee who worked for as long as 110 hours a week and died of a heart attack at the age of 34. Another was that of a 22-year old nurse who died from a heart attack, after 34 hours of continuous duty five times a month[1]. The extreme physical and mental pressure created by overworking is now recognized as a global problem. Heart attack and stroke due to stress and a starvation diet are the major medical causes of Karoshi deaths[2]

Another equally disconcerting phenomenon is suicide from overworking and stressful working conditions. The Japanese word for this is **Karojisatsu**. Karojisatsu results from 'long work hours, heavy workloads, lack of job control, routine and repetitive tasks, interpersonal conflicts, inadequate rewards, employment insecurity, and organizational problems could become psychosocial hazards at work.'[3]

We are conscious and intelligent creatures. Our health and our happiness are our most valuable gifts. Still, we choose to exchange our most valuable assets for a lifestyle that drains and destroys them both.

The challenge is that we often don't know that we are on that path of destruction. A friend once told me that when there is more than one person in a room, there is bound to be suffering. Perhaps we do not need another person in the room for suffering to happen. We can suffer without anyone's help. What is often missing is the capacity to pause and realize that we are suffering and that our suffering is optional. We need to recognize that we can choose to escape from suffering in ways that are pragmatic as they are effective. And, we can choose to alleviate the sufferings of those around us in our workspaces. We can do this any day, every day. This is the choice of compassion.

Compassion is a multifaceted human response to suffering. In the workplace, compassion *is simply being able to make the right choice to alleviate suffering and balancing those choices with wisdom*. Compassion is evolutionarily hard-wired into us. Often we only need to recognize that we **can** act with compassion, and permit ourselves to do so.

In the context of the workplace, compassion translates into a fearless desire for all-around success. Compassion allows us to create success for ourselves, our colleagues, our organizations, and the customers we serve. Cultural narratives, lack of awareness of suffering, and fear often block compassion. But these are blocks that can be easily overcome. Compassion is a muscle that can be strengthened with practice. In the coming chapters, we will explore the why, what and when of compassion, discuss the science of compassion, and understand why compassion matters in workplaces. We will then do a deep dive of nine pragmatic life skills that come together as pillars upholding a personal and cultural framework of compassion. The final sections of the book explore how we can apply compassion skills to address real-life challenges, create organizational shifts, and create a vision for a happier future.

Industrial Revolutions

We are in the middle of the fourth industrial revolution. The first industrial revolution, dating to the end of the 18th century, witnessed the emergence of mechanization using steam power. The second industrial revolution, which started toward the end of the 19th century, utilized a new form of energy- electricity - for mass production, and allowed for the division of labor. The third industrial revolution, dating to the latter half of the 20th century, utilized electronics and computers to automate manufacturing. The ongoing fourth industrial revolution aims to integrate our physical and virtual worlds to create globally connected factories.

With all the emphasis on production and productivity, it is easy to overlook *the human motivations of the industrial revolutions.* I believe that all of the industrial revolutions had the same underlying human needs- a need for fair access to resources, a need to flatten out limiting social hierarchies, and a desire for improved human health and happiness. Even with the clumsiness and callousness with which we have wielded the tools of the industrial revolutions, the quality of life has undoubtedly increased since the revolutions began. Resources, knowledge, opportunities for connection and equality, access to happiness tools are at an all-time high. But the truth remains that we are still an unhappy generation, and the tools that were meant to ease life and make us happy are only making us stressed and depressed.

What I believe is happening is that we have stocked up the refrigerator with vegetables that we don't know how to cook. What we need is not more physical or digital resources, but tools that can help us consume the fruits of the industrial revolutions in ways that will make us happy. These tools are tools of the mind and heart. More technology, more digitalization, is not going to make us happier. We need to return to our roots- and develop personal skills that nurture happiness. This is the fifth revolution as I see it- a rediscovery of tools and skills that make us uniquely human. While steam, electricity, electronics, and artificial intelligence have powered the other industrial revolutions, the fifth one will be powered by the human spirit.

The fifth revolution is superbly on target to elevate human progress and happiness at the same time. And I believe that *the fifth revolution, while universally applicable, will find their ground-zero in workplaces.* As we will discuss in the following pages, there is no shortage of suffering in workplaces. Our current paradigm for success is skewed. We wander into work, become temporary automatons, meet short-term goals, collect paychecks, and pick our personalities up on the way out. In the process, the best of our potential lies unrecognized and unused. Therefore, we lose purpose, become stressed and distressed, and become unhappy. We deserve better. We deserve an internal and cultural framework in workplaces that allows us to flourish both personally and professionally. Workplaces that bring out the best in people thrive. The fifth revolution starts with creating these workplaces. The fifth revolution has a secret sauce. That secret sauce is compassion. Compassion, practiced by individuals and organizations, will maximize our capacity to consume the fruits of the industrial revolution in ways that elevate happiness and efficiency.

About this book

This book is designed to challenge and inspire individuals and organizations to become compassionate by 'looking inside' to 'shift outside'. I trust you will find all the workplace compassion tools and skills in these pages. So, this is my invitation: to discover your personal capacity to be compassionate to yourself and all the people in your world, starting with your workplace.

After all, *all global transformations start as a transformation of the human spirit.*

'The Fifth Revolution' has stories, perspectives, exercises, assessments, affirmations and more. These are meant to inspire, challenge and nudge you toward a happier, kinder lifestyle and work setting. The image below shows the five key intentions of the book.

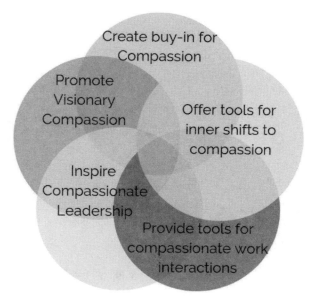

I hope that this book seeds a revolution of human compassion in workplaces. But there can be no revolution without **you**!

As Ursula K. Le Guin says, *"You cannot buy the revolution. You cannot make the revolution. You can only be the revolution, it is in your spirit, or it is nowhere."*

I invite you to be a part of the revolution by experimenting with your learnings from this book. If you feel compelled to inspire others, you can share your stories and perspectives at **www.FifthRevolution.life.**

Onward to The Fifth Revolution!

SELF-REFLECTION

Before you start reading this book, please try this short self-reflective exercise. List out five human challenges that you are currently experiencing at work (for example, stress, connection, communication, anxiety, leadership challenges).

In Column A, indicate how intense the challenge is for you at this time, in a rating scale from 1 to 5. 1 is minimal emotional stress, and 5 is as painful as it gets. After you have completed the book and had a chance to experiment with some of the concepts you have learned, revisit this page and complete Column B. Observe what has changed.

	My greatest human challenges at work	As I start this book Column A	After experiments with compassion Column B
1		Rating: Notes:	Rating: Notes:
2		Rating: Notes:	Rating: Notes:

3		Rating: Notes:	Rating: Notes:
4		Rating: Notes:	Rating: Notes:
5		Rating: Notes:	Rating: Notes:

SECTION 1:
UNDERSTANDING COMPASSION

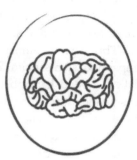

What
Why
When
Where

Understanding Compassion

Compassion is our innate capacity to alleviate suffering. The word suffering can be construed as many different things. For the purposes of understanding compassion, suffering is any event that disrupts harmony, causes dis-ease and dissonance. Life is strife with pain. The loss of a loved one and the loss of a favorite pen can both cause suffering. It is how the mind perceives and reacts to the incidents that happen to us that define the magnitude of pain. Therefore, it is not realistic to compare suffering. What is real, though, is that as observers of suffering, we can try to alleviate it. This is what compassion is about.

Compassion stems from an evolutionary desire for personal and social safety and harmony. When we see suffering, a part of our brain starts identifying ourselves with the person who is suffering. There is an urge to alleviate it. When we do so, we feel good. We have added to the evolutionary karma. An act of compassion has happened. But we don't always see suffering. Perhaps because there is so much suffering around us, we learn not to notice it. Not noticing suffering avoids personal distress.

In September 2000, a young man named Kevin Hines jumped off the Golden Gate Bridge in San Francisco. Before he jumped, he paced the bridge, fighting the inner demons that were telling him to jump. A lady came up to him and asked him to take her photograph. He did. She did not even notice the anguish in the person behind the camera. Kevin is only one of three people who have survived a jump from the bridge. "I said to myself," Kevin recollected later. "If one person comes up to me and says, 'Are you okay? Is something wrong? Can I help you?' I was going to tell them my whole life story, and they were going to make me safe."

Sometimes we notice suffering, but our experiences tell us that we do not have to be the ones alleviating the suffering. When we fail to relieve the suffering that we notice, we feel bad. We create internal chatter. We disavow responsibility by saying 'they deserve the suffering because...' This makes us feel better because now we have judgments about the other person that justifies their suffering. Therefore, we do not have to feel their pain.

Another common way compassion opportunities are missed is when we pass on the responsibility of kindness to the collective commons. The narrative here is 'I see suffering, but lots of others see the same suffering too. Someone else is going to address it'.

Not noticing the suffering around us, and judgments, which stop us from feeling the suffering of the other, essentially block compassion. But imagine what happens when more and more members of a community stop being compassionate. Without the fundamental safety net of compassion, a society loses its evolutionary edge. There is infighting, social distress, unethical behaviors, and overall disruption of harmony. His Holiness the Dalai Lama said, *Love and compassion are necessities, not luxuries. Without them, humanity cannot survive.*

This is what Charles Darwin said in his book, The Descent of Man and Selection in Relation to Sex: *"Sympathy will have been increased through natural selection,"* Darwin wrote, *"for those communities which include the greatest number of the most sympathetic members, would flourish best, and rear the greatest number of offspring."* Darwin used the word sympathy to indicate compassion.

The necessity of compassion is real for organizations as it is for our species.

Researchers break down the compassion process into four steps.

1. Noticing suffering
2. Feeling for the sufferer
3. Suspending judgment
4. Moving toward action

In other words, compassionate responses stem from awareness, openness to looking at people without the baggage of judgment, and making a choice to do something about it.

Sometimes we are able to react to situations with compassion; sometimes we are not able to do so. Our mental and physical health at any given time, our sense of fulfilment and abundance, our current personal struggle, how others have treated us, our inner capacity to handle suffering-so many factors go into determining whether we meet situations with compassion or non-compassion. Sometimes we catch ourselves reacting non-compassionately to situations, when we clearly know that we could be reacting compassionately. Those are times when we have to acknowledge our own humanness. We may be responding to not only the situation at hand, but an accumulation of several triggers that have not been resolved. Like death by a thousand papercuts, it is typically the accumulation of many unaddressed challenges that evoke discompassionate outbursts.

However, when we have the awareness and possibility of compassion at the top of our minds, we can more regularly act with compassion. This comes from learning and creating compassion habits. Accumulation of small acts of compassion prevents painful outbursts that cause suffering for ourselves and others. We will focus on the how-tos of creating compassion habits in the next part of this book.

One of the critical elements of compassion is the ability to operate without judgment. This is also one of the most challenging things to do. We judge people because we are habituated to relative thinking. We need frameworks to compare and make decisions. If we do not have anything to compare people to, we have to expend that much more mental real estate in decision making. Judgments are also self-preservation tools, protecting us from getting hurt. We create mental bins to put people, which allows us to act quickly and effectively in our interactions with them. Without judgments, we will continuously be stumbling and being mowed over.

Since judgments typically start from a place of fear and scarcity, they can be hurtful. When we see a person who is in the street looking disheveled and smelly, we may immediately assume that this person will ask us for money. So we avoid this person's gaze and walk in the opposite direction. We make decisions about people when we do not even know them. We then use that unfounded bias to interface al. It is said that *it takes 7 seconds to form 11 impressions about someone and 10 interactions to the contrary to change that impression*[1]. Since judgments are knee jerk responses and may not involve executive brain functions, we may end up in action that we regret.

You will find ideas for suspending judgments scattered throughout the book, as part of other compassion tools. The key thing to remember is that judgments are sticky. We can become stuck if we do not balance between judgments that protect us and judgments that make us discompassionate.

Before we move any further with discussing compassion, we need to clarify what compassion is and what it is not. As an evangelist of workplace compassion, I have encountered a lot of resistance to the idea of compassion, and much of it comes from a place where compassion is misunderstood.

Compassion facts and myths

1. Compassion is not a religious experience. Non-human animals, which do not practice religion, also exhibit compassion. Compassion is an innate response to suffering, as we discussed earlier.

2. Compassion is not just a nice to have. Many people tend to downplay compassion as a fuzzy skill or a new age concept. The truth is, nothing can be more fundamental to success in business and personal relationships than the ability to create trust and safety by supporting each other in times of need.

3. Compassionate acts do not have to be grand gestures. Small everyday challenges (micro-suffering) are prevalent, and so the opportunities to relieve these are abundant as well (micro-compassion).

4. Compassion does not necessarily have to be reactive as a response to suffering. It can be proactive. By practicing compassionate behaviors, we can prevent suffering from happening in the first place.

5. Compassion is not a weakness. In the context of leadership, it could perhaps be the most admired leadership qual-

ity. Some of the very successful business leaders of our time espouse compassion as a critical component of a successful business.

6. Compassion is not a carpet mindset. Compassion can be and is often fierce. It involves making tough decisions, being fearlessly vulnerable, and bravely stepping into the mire to relieve challenges as needed. New York Times bestselling author and meditation teacher, Sharon Salzberg says, *"We can learn the art of fierce compassion - redefining strength, deconstructing isolation and renewing a sense of community, practicing letting go of rigid 'us' vs. 'them' thinking, while cultivating power and clarity in response to stressful situations."*

7. Compassion can be learned. As the Hebb's rule states, 'neurons that fire together wire together.' As we incorporate compassion habits as part of everyday living, we gain greater access to making compassionate choices when situations demand.

    And finally...

8. Suffering is universal. Small or big, it feels good when our suffering is noticed, and someone feels for us, someone wants to help us. So compassion is universal, just as suffering is universal, irrespective of race, gender, and physical differences.

However, compassion is often confused with two other words- *empathy and sympathy.* Let us look at the differences in responses to human suffering.

Imagine a scenario where you and a friend are walking on a lonely road. Suddenly you see a big hole in the middle of the road. Your friend fails to see the hole, and he falls into it. He is screaming for help. What would you do?

You could walk away from there. This is not your problem. Your friend should have been more careful. This is apathy.

You could look down into the pit and tell him how sorry you are and how much you wish he had not fallen into the hole. This is sympathy.

You might feel great pain for your friend. Your mirror neurons are firing, and you are feeling his suffering intensely. You jump into the hole yourself. This is empathy.

You see your friend suffering. You feel a great urge to help him. You are not judging your friend by past experiences. Right now, he is suffering. You know you cannot lift him out by yourself. You ask your friend to wait, and you rush to find someone who can help. This is compassion.

Responses to suffering

Imagine you are walking on a lonely road with a friend. There is a pit in the middle of the road. Your friend falls into the pit. How will you respond?

Apathy and Sympathy are disempowering. Empathy is unsustainable. When you jumped into the pit to be with your friend, you lost your capacity to help your friend. Also, another big challenge with empathy is the fatigue that comes with it. This is the burnout we see in caregivers and medical workers, for example. In psychology, Theory of Mind refers to our ability to understand the mental states of others and realize that the mental states of others might be different from our own. This self vs. others difference sometimes gets blurred in the face of witnessing suffering, and therefore people ascribe the sufferings of others as their own. This state is called **empathic distress**. However, compassion came from a place of wanting to relieve the suffering, not identifying with it. For this reason, *compassion is both empowering and sustainable.*

Compassion and empathy are different, even at a biological level. Research from the lab of Tania Singer indicates that different parts of the brain associated with different parts of the brain are activated by empathy vs. compassion training. Also, they were able to show that people with compassion training ended up feeling kinder and more eager to help others than those with empathy training[2].

Science of Compassion

Just a few years ago, compassion was a scientifically intangible trait. Just as we know that we are alive but cannot point out what life is, we knew our propensity for compassion, but could not pinpoint the biological basis for it. In the past few years, though, researchers have taken a multi-pronged approach to dissect compassion. One line of research is to understand the parts of the brain and the neural pathways associated with compassionate behaviors. The other is to understand the neurochemicals that drive compassion.

Functional magnetic resonance imaging or fMRI is a tool, which measures which parts of the brain are active by detecting changes associated with blood flow. When there is more blood flow to a particular part of the brain, it lights up in brain scans. The blood flow correlates to brain activity in that region. fMRI is very helpful in studies linking brain activity to simulated compassion. Richard Davidson and others have demonstrated that a two-week practice of loving-kindness meditation (which we will discuss in the coming chapters) reduces the responses of the amygdala, which is the fight or flight part of the brain[3].

Tania Singer and Kim Olimecki did meta-analyses on empathy for pain fMRI studies which revealed that "a portion of the anterior insula and a specific part of the anterior cingulate cortex were consistently activated, both during the experience of pain as well as when vicariously feeling with the suffering of others[4].

The anterior cingulate cortex, as we will see later, is a part that also lights up during experiences of gratitude. These experiments help give a physical dimension to a behavioral trait.

Vagus nerve and compassion

The Vagus nerve (vagus is wandering in Latin) is a long bundle of nerves that begins in the brain and controls the parasympathetic nervous system (PNS) which regulates relaxation. The PNS balances the Sympathetic nervous system (SNS), which allows us to handle emergencies through fight or flight responses. The Vagus nerve regulates a myriad of functions including immune regulation and stem cell activation. Because of its role in controlling the relaxation response through the PNS, altering the Vagus response can help regulate the levels of stress. The Vagus nerve regulates Acetylcholine, a chemical that helps to regulate neural signals, thereby controlling inflammation response.

The vagus nerve has been dubbed as the 'nerve of compassion' because when activated, it helps create feelings of compassion, happiness, gratitude, and love. One of the ways this happens is through the regulation of oxytocin, a molecule, which is critical for our compassion responses[5]. The Vagus nerve is also associated with feelings of caretaking and recognition of common humanity. Dr. Nancy Eisenberg at Arizona State University showed that young children show that children with baseline activity of the Vagus nerve are more likely to be cooperative and giving[6]. Dr. Dacher

Keltner at the Greater Good Center, University of Berkley, calls people with high baseline Vagus nerve activity, as Vagal superstars.

There is plenty of proof for the Vagus nerve plays a vital role in the mind-body nexus. Activating the Vagus nerve can reduce stress; bring down inflammation and host of other good things, including improving heart health[7]. Given these, there is an active interest in understanding how one can activate the vagus nerve.

Research shows that regulated breathing exercises like pranayama, long exhalation to inhalation time ratio in breathing, can improve our Vagus profile. Fredrickson and Kok from the Max Planck Institute demonstrate that social connection that activates Vagal tone[8]. Dr. Keltner's research shows that subjects exposed to images of suffering have increased vagal activity. The more compassion we feel, the more the Vagus activity[9]. Compassion tools that we discuss in the book - loving-kindness meditation, self-compassion, mindful breathing, and perspective-taking are practices that improve our vagal activity.

Neurochemistry of compassion

Neurochemicals are small organic molecules or peptides (short protein sequences) that transmit signals between neurons and help promote the growth and repair of nerve cells.

Dr. Loretta Breuning is a **Professor Emerita of Management at California State University** and the **Founder of Inner Mammal Institute**. She studies human motivation and neurochemicals that drive our behaviors. Below, she discusses the chemicals that wire us.

"This brain we've inherited is not easy to manage. It's the challenge that comes with the gift of life. Natural selection built a brain that's focused on its survival. It releases chemicals that feel good (dopamine, serotonin, oxytocin, endorphin) when it sees a way to meet a survival need or relieve a survival threat. But our brain defines survival in a quirky way: it cares about the survival of your genes, and it relies on neural pathways built in youth. Compassion triggers a good feeling when we connect it to our survival in one way or another. You don't consciously think that, of course, but your happy chemicals are controlled by brain structures that do not rely on conscious thought. Let's take a closer look at the brain that makes compassion feel good.

You have inherited your brain from survivors. This may sound obvious, but it's sort of a miracle when you think about it: survival rates are low in the state of nature, yet your ancestors did what it took to make babies and keep them alive long enough to make babies going back millions of years. Your ancestors survived because they evolved a brain that rewards survival behavior with a good feeling. Life was extremely harsh, but each individual kept taking steps toward meeting their needs because the steps stimulated happy chemicals. We have inherited these chemicals from earlier animals, and they're controlled by brain structures that all mammals have in common (such as the amygdala, hippocampus, hypothalamus, and lower parts often called the "reptile brain"). The mammal brain does not process language, so it does not tell you in words when it reacts to the threats and opportunities around you.

All mammals have a cortex too, but size matters when it comes to the cortex. We, humans, have a vast reserve of extra neurons that can create abstractions. This enables you to tell yourself in words that you are not interested in your survival, and you only care about the needs of others. Your mammal brain keeps doing the job it evolved to do, and if caring about others builds social alliances, that promotes survival and your mammal brain rewards you with happy chemicals. If others fail to show concern for your welfare that you expect, your mammal brain sees that as a survival threat and alerts you with an unhappy chemical (cortisol).

Your two brains work together to promote your survival. If you let your mammal brain run wild, you may feel good at the moment about things that hurt you in the long run. But if you ignore your mammal brain, you will not feel happy because the cortex does not control the chemicals. Let's see how each of the happy chemicals rewards behaviors that help meet survival needs, including compassionate behavior. But first, we must know how our unique individual neural pathways control these chemicals. You were born with billions of neurons but very few connections between them. You built connections each time you activated a neural pathway. You strengthened those pathways each time you released neurochemicals. Good and bad feelings wire a brain to repeat behaviors expected to feel good and avoid behaviors expected to feel bad. The pathways you built before age eight, and during puberty, became the superhighways of your brain because myelin is abundant in those years. Myelin coats neurons so they conduct electricity at super speeds. Whatever you think or do with your myelinated neurons feels natural and normal.

One experience wired into the core of every one of us is the extreme vulnerability of youth. We, humans, are far more helpless at birth than our animal ancestors. There's a direct correlation between the size of a creature's brain and the length of its childhood. Lizards have no childhood at all. They leave home the instant they crack out of their shell, and if they don't leave fast enough, a parent eats them. They are born pre-wired with the survival knowledge of their ancestors. Their survival skills are limited, so only about 5% of them survive, but a mother lizard can make thousands of babies, so the species survives. A mammal cannot do that because warm-blooded babies are so hard to gestate. We mammals put our eggs in very few baskets, and then do our best to keep each one alive. Attachment is the key to survival for creatures born unwired. The bigger a mammal's brain, the longer the attachment period.

Let's look at attachment from the newborn brain's perspective. A human baby has needs it cannot meet, so it surges with cortisol, the threat chemical. Cortisol triggers crying, one of our few hard-wired behaviors. Crying brings relief, but soon, a baby feels more needs and more cortisol. We start our lives with an urgent sense of threat, which motivates us to act to relieve it. Before a baby knows what a mother is, or even knows what milk is, it knows that relief is at hand when it hears certain sounds. Each time its needs are met, neurons connect, and expectations are built. Gradually we learn a wide range of strategies for meeting our needs instead of just crying. We learn to interact with others in ways that promote our survival. These interactions feel good because they stimulate dopamine, serotonin, and/or oxytocin.

Oxytocin creates a pleasant feeling of trust. Reptiles only release it during sex and avoid other reptiles the rest of the time.

Mammals like company. We are born with a surge of oxytocin because this chemical triggers labor contractions and lactation in addition to the pleasure of social trust. So we are born ready to trust, but the oxytocin is metabolized in a few minutes. Touch stimulates more of it, which is why animals lick their babies and primates cuddle them. Touch and trust always go together in the state of nature because an individual close enough to touch you is close enough to hurt you. It would be nice to enjoy a steady flow of oxytocin all the time, but trusting everyone does not promote survival. We have inherited a brain that makes careful decisions about when to release the good feeling. It does that by connecting neurons whenever oxytocin flows. The neural circuits built from experience wire a young mammal to transfer its attachment from its mother to a herd or pack or troop or tribe.

Oxytocin rewards you with a good feeling when you build social alliances because safety in numbers promotes survival in the state of nature. But oxytocin is soon metabolized, and you have to do more to get more. If you distance yourself from the herd, your oxytocin falls, and it feels unsafe. This response helps young mammals survive without having to experience the jaws of a predator first hand. But we humans do not want to stick with the herd all the time. We want to check out greener pastures because that stimulates dopamine. Thus we live with the frustrating tension between the dopamine of discovering new rewards and the oxytocin of social support. Compassion can help us stimulate the oxytocin of social bonds while we are out exploring new pastures. Compassion stimulates the good feeling of trust despite all the many reasons not to. Compassion frees us to leave our tribe and still stimulate that much-desired tribal feeling.

Dopamine creates a good feeling that you are about to meet a need. It is triggered by the taste of milk in a newborn baby's mouth. Each time a need is met, dopamine bridges all the neurons active at that moment. This wires us to turn on the exciting feeling the next time we see something similar. Dopamine releases the reserve tank of energy. It tells the body that an expected reward is worth an investment of effort. Thus, the quest to feel good motivates a body to do what it takes to meet its needs in ways that worked before. Our ancestors had to forage constantly to survive, and dopamine motivated them to seek before they were weakened by hunger. In the modern world, our basic needs are easily met, so we have to keep looking for ways to stimulate our dopamine. Compassion is one way to relieve this conundrum. When we help others achieve their needs, our mirror neurons stimulate the good feeling of meeting our own needs.

Our brains evolved to seek the good feeling of serotonin as well. Serotonin is a complex chemical found in mammals, reptiles, fish, mollusks, and even amoeba. Serotonin prepares the digestive system for food. Group-living creatures have a complex response to food because every tasty morsel you see is usually seen by another. If two mammals rush toward the same banana, the weaker individual will get hurt. Thus, mammals evolved a brain that compares itself to others before it reaches for food. When it sees that it's in the weaker position, it releases cortisol and withdraws. When it sees that it's in the stronger position, serotonin is released, and it asserts. A mammal that never asserts will fail to pass on its genes. You could not descend from that mammal. You have inherited a brain that seeks serotonin. It's not aggression but the calm sense that you have the power to satisfy your needs. Alas, each serotonin spurt is quickly metabolized, and you have to do more to get more.

Academics and journalists do not acknowledge this information about serotonin; they report that animals share food by contriving artificial laboratory situations and omitting evidence to the contrary. But every farmer and field biologist knows that stronger animals bite and claw weaker individuals who get in their way. Fights are avoided because weaker mammals learn from a very young age that self-restraint feels better than being bitten. Natural selection built a brain skilled at making these social judgments. We humans learn to restrain the urge to grab, bite, or claw, whether we are stronger or weaker. We learn the risk of being ostracized from the group and losing out on oxytocin. But we still crave the good feeling of serotonin, so we are left to juggle complex trade-offs. Compassion is an effective solution because you get to enjoy the stronger position without the risk of conflict. Many people rely on the feeling of moral superiority to stimulate their serotonin. They continually compare themselves to those they deem less compassionate and come out on top. It's frustrating, but it's better than biting and scratching.

The mammalian urge for social dominance is easy to see in others, but hard to see in yourself. It's comfortable to believe that "our society is the problem" and an alternative society will eliminate this natural impulse. I learned this as a student and passed it on as a teacher. I participated in the distortion of facts to stay safely within the herd of academic consensus. Here's a simple example of that distortion. Zookeepers know that if they leave food out in the open, weaker individuals get injured or starve. So they've developed a technique called "cooperative feeding," which employs two keepers – one continually feeding the alpha while the other feeds the rest of the group. Calling this "cooperation" masks the inconvenient truth about the natural urge for self-assertion. If you acknowledge this truth, you can lose your membership in the warm and fuzzy herd.

Modern medicine has created the belief that everyone can have a constant flow of serotonin just from sitting on the couch. Academics and journalists have created the idea that everyone would be happy all the time if the right political policies were embraced. Licensed credentialed professionals cannot question these beliefs without risking their credentials. I have compassion for them. But each of us has power over our own brain. Distorting your true nature will not help you understand your neurochemical ups and downs. You can be compassionate and also accept your authentic inner mammal and the inner mammal of your fellow homo sapiens.

Indeed, authenticity favors compassion. It helps you understand why other people are the way they are. It's not easy having a huge cortex attached to a mammalian operating system that wires itself in youth. But you can meet your needs and enjoy helping others meet their needs. You can celebrate your ability to avoid conflict, and the cortisol alarm it triggers. You can feel good when your two brains work together instead of feeling inadequate and blaming society.

Our neurochemical dilemmas are frustrating, but they are not new. Fifty million years ago, monkeys lived with the same frustrations. We have inherited a brain that longs to feel important because that stimulates serotonin. It wants to find new resources because that stimulates dopamine. It longs for safety in numbers because that stimulates oxytocin. This brain makes you feel like your survival is threatened when you see obstacles to these needs. It's not easy being a mammal, but you can celebrate the survival power of your brain instead of cynically condemning your natural impulses. This is self-compassion. **"**

"Today's science is tomorrow's technology."
— Edward Teller, The Legacy Of Hiroshima

The science of compassion is evolving rapidly. There are increasingly more tools and interest to dissect the 'humanity' in us humans. All of this could mean new opportunities for action.

For example, science is teaching us that the gut microbiome (which is the microbial constitution of our guts) impacts the vagal nerve function and our emotional states[10]. Our diet influences our gut microbiome. There might soon be a time where we can create a 'compassion diet'.

Companies are trying to create neural interfaces that can alter brain functions. Some companies are even exploring the possibilities of brain chips that can create a human-machine symbiosis. Perhaps in the future, we will understand the neurophysiology of the brain well enough to develop machine-based compassion interventions. Maybe that would usher in an age of peace, without wars, without boundaries, without the need to fear each other.

Until then, we have the tools of meditation and behavior-based modifications (as this book aims to inspire) to kick-start a revolution of compassion.

Balancing compassion and wisdom

Just as a bird needs two wings to move forward, compassion must be balanced with wisdom to be sustainable. The wisdom component of compassion stems from knowing oneself and asking hard questions. Even though the process of wisdom-testing a compassionate response seems cerebral and drawn out, with time, it becomes intuitive and immediate. As compassion teachers point out, compassion without wisdom is mushy, and wisdom without compassion is hard. The balance between compassion and wisdom is where the sweet spot of sustained kindness lies.

Wisdom in a compassionate response could involve some essential considerations:

1. Is my compassion balanced? Does my compassion for others also include compassion for myself? In other words, am I giving at the cost of myself, which will make my compassion unsustainable?

2. What is the intent of my compassionate response? Do I have personal expectations from my act of compassion? If my focus is not entirely on the suffering and its alleviation, but turned toward personal gain, how sustainable will my actions be when I do not get what I want?

3. What kind of judgments will arise that will stop me from being compassionate in the future?

4. Does my act of compassion pass the W4 test: why, who, where, and when. Knowing this will help me avoid becoming a doormat giver.

Balancing Wisdom and Compassion

Sustainable Compassion	Unsustainable compassion
1 Has clarity about the problem and personal role in solution	Problem and personal role not fully considered
2 Understands self limitations	Inflated opinion of persoanl capacity to help
3 Big pciture thinking	Short term thinking
4 Understands the who, why and when of compassion	Knee jerk reacion to suffering
5 Understands where compassion interferes with self compassion	Compassion stretches into self-compassion
6 Is not grounded in guilt.	Persists through guilt
7 Creates emotional space between action and expectations	Involves emotional entanglement
8 Is not afraid to say no and set boundaries	Is afraid to say no and set boundaries

It is easy to become overwhelmed by the suffering around us. It becomes imperative, therefore, to realize our limitations for compassion, and do so without judgment.

Imagine that you are walking on a perfectly clean street. Then you see a brick in the middle of the street. You are worried someone might stumble on the stone. You pick the brick and throw it away. You feel good. Imagine now that the street is littered with bricks. If you start removing every stone out of the way, you will feel burnt out soon. You feel overwhelmed, but also guilty. A compassionate response is realizing your limitations and accepting that you cannot remove all the bricks in the street. It is indeed compassionate to only do what you can, and feel happy knowing that even a single brick you have moved out of the way has helped someone. Another compassionate response is to think abundantly and inspire others to start a clean-up movement, which will collectively achieve what you, as an individual, cannot.

Even more difficult to practice, but still as compassionate, is knowing that sometimes the best response is to not act. Not everything needs fixing. Sometimes compassion requires your courageous presence and nothing else. Accepting that your inaction comes from a place of consideration, not callousness, could be an act of compassion.

Dr. James R. Doty, MD, is a **Clinical Professor in the Department of Neurosurgery at Stanford University School of Medicine**. He is also the **Founder and Director of the Center for Compassion and Altruism Research and Education at Stanford University** and the author of the wildly successful book, **Into the Magic Shop.**

"There are several people who feel that if one is compassionate, it implies that they are a pushover to be used and stepped on in the business environment." Dr. Doty says. "There are some people who will use the term compassion in terms of description of themselves, but unfortunately, that is not what they mean. What they are saying is that they do not have the resolve and fortitude, and the strength to stand up to bullies, narcissists, or selfish people. A compassionate person knows his or her boundaries, what they are willing to accept, what is reasonable and fair. They do not let individuals extend beyond those boundaries. In interactions with others, they certainly have an openness and non-judgmental attitude, but that is also tempered with the pragmatic and realistic, and being able to be direct. So if you are really compassionate and someone is taking obvious advantage of you, you know they are not a floor mat that people step on. You tell them that it is unacceptable and that you will not allow that and you will not have further interactions with them if that is how they are going to behave. You are not being mean to them; you are being compassionate by being direct, forthright, and by protecting yourself. Being helpless and being compassionate are two different things. One comes from a place of insecurity and a lack of compassion for self. The other is a manifestation of being kind to yourself, knowing who you are and treating yourself well, which means you do not allow others to 'step-on' you. Unfortunately, there is a subset of people in the business world who believe that insecure people, people who are afraid, are people to step on and take advantage of in their path forward in their careers.

In my own case, I had an individual who I supervised, who was not performing. Certainly, I was empathetic to this person's situation. As a leader, my job is to help individuals flourish and thrive and to maximize their potential in the context of their work environment. But regardless of how much I tried to help this person, unfortunately, she did not make an effort to improve and frankly she was also a manipulative person. I fired her. I told her that at least in the context of her job performance under my supervision she was not performing, that I had tried various ways to assist and since this was not effective, it was not appropriate to continue her employment. And then I wished her the best and let her go. I do not feel bad about that at all. I knew I tried to be nonjudgmental, I had tried to be accepting, I openly and honestly and transparently described her deficiencies, defined a path to address those, and she chose not to participate. So, I think firing her was the most compassionate thing to do. This is different from a situation where you feel threatened by an employee who is a threat to your position, and you try to undermine them. **"**

Compassion hurdles

Several limiting beliefs block expressions and reception of compassion. A limiting belief is like a thin rope that ties an elephant. When the elephant is small, the rope is strong enough to hold her back. She tugs and pulls in vain and eventually gives up. When she is older and stronger, the elephant can easily break the rope, but her past experiences of failure now limit her, and she doesn't even try to break free from the rope.

One of the ways to effectively address a limiting belief is to look at in the face and ask, 'How true if this belief?'' Limiting beliefs tend to crumble in the face of fearless, direct questioning. So the introspection to be made is this: 'Knowing what I know about being compassionate, what are my limiting beliefs about being compassionate?' And then proceed to question the validity of those limiting beliefs.

Another reality to contend with is that it is easier to be compassionate when things are going well. It is so much more difficult when we are being triggered. **Dr. James R.Doty** shares this about choosing compassion when being triggered.

"This is one of the more difficult challenges. In the work environment, your sympathetic nervous system, which is your fight or flight response, is triggered, and you have stress and anxiety. When you are in that situation, which many people in workplaces are, the executive functions of the brain are impaired. Therefore, you are not as thoughtful; you do not have access to past experiences; you are not as discerning because you are making a quick decision through the fight or flight response that was engaged. As Viktor Frankl shares, your freedom is in the space between the stimulus and the response. When you are threatened, you could consciously step back and count slowly 1,2, 3, 4, 5, 6… and the very act of doing this allows time for your executive functions to make more thoughtful decisions. In the business environment, you are confronted with this frequently.

As an example, I was working on a project with another physician. He worked at a different company, but we were friends, and we were working on this project together. One day he walked into my office for a meeting, and he was almost rude, very abrupt and frankly, aggressive. It was shocking to me because that is not his nature. My normal response would be to react accordingly. When somebody comes at you aggressively, your fight or flight response results in us fighting them or confronting them and be equally aggressive and rude. For a microsecond, I thought about that. But then I paused for a few seconds and said to myself, 'Why would this person be doing this? This is not their usual behavior' So instead of being confrontational and aggressive to this person, I said to him. "This isn't you talking. There is something else going on here." And with this, he burst into tears. What had happened was that he had been terminated from his primary job. He was young and had young children, so trying to save money, he had decided to forgo an extension of his health insurance. But then his wife had gone to the doctor and found that she had breast cancer. Now they had no insurance for her situation. His response toward me had nothing to do with me. His response was brought on by his own fear and anxiety about his future.

Often we interact with people, and we believe that the nature of that conversation or the tone of that conversation relates to the events at hand, when in many cases, that is not true at all. Studies on free will show that our actions in the world are unrelated to what is happening at a conscious level. So we believe that our interactions are a manifestation of the conscious us, when in fact the majority of the time, maybe even 90% of the time or more, it is a manifestation of events going on at an unconscious level. As an example, you are driving along with your car windows rolled down. Suddenly you feel hungry and make a statement that you are starved. What actually has happened is you got the whiff of cooking from a restaurant, and you translated this that you were hungry when in fact you were not hungry at all. This is the nature of something called 'priming'. And priming occurs at an unconscious level, but it determines your actions. For many people, those actions are retroactively defined as us making those decisions.

One of the tools that has come in handy for me to stay centered is the **'Alphabets of the Heart'**. I use this as my daily practice. It has helped me as a physician and as a human being. When I wake up, I sit on the side of the bed and pause a few seconds, and breathe in and out slowly, and I appreciate my presence in the world and the awe of the very nature of the universe. Then with intention, I go over each of the ten letters in the tool kit. It starts with C and goes through L.

C- Compassion for Self and Others. If you cannot be kind to yourself, it is difficult to give love to others.

D- Dignity. Recognizing the dignity of every person. No one is better than you, or worse than you. We are all equal. Before you can give true compassion, you should be able to look at them eye to eye, not look down upon them.

E- Equanimity. We all have ups and downs in life. Equanimity is to keep evenness of temperament through our ups and downs. If we try to hold on to that feeling of up or down, we are terminally unhappy. The ups, while wonderful, are transitory. It is not that you do not enjoy your times when everything is great, and you are happy. It is just that you do not get lost in them and grasping for them all the time.

Conversely, times of downs are also transitory. They can be extraordinarily painful when they happen. But when you look back and reflect, you find these are often the times which resulted in the greatest insights and wisdom and strengths in your life.

F- Forgiveness. While others have wronged us, each of us has wronged another person. Holding on to the anger toward another does nothing to the other person and does not help you. Being able to forgive is not to forget, but allowing the anger you carry, to dissipate. If someone hurts me and I forgive them, I carry no anger toward them. I will be polite to them, but I am not going to engage in further business or interactions with them, and I am certainly not going to be angry at them, because it hurts me and stops me from being my best self.

G- Gratitude. To recognize that we have so much to be grateful for.

H- Humility. This also relates to dignity. It doesn't matter that you are accomplished. What matters is your heart and how open you are to learning. Making judgments about how big or important you are, are false narratives that only make one unhappy and create jealousy. You can always tell how good a doctor is by watching them walk down the hallway. A good doctor knows the names of the nurses, acknowledges the janitorial staff, acknowledges the people who change the sheets and knows that he cannot do his job successfully in his area without the help and support of everyone around him or her. This is in contrast to others who walk around with an air of self-importance, are brusque, demanding, and don't acknowledge certain people. We, unfortunately, see this quite frequently in business settings and among physicians. We are all equal; we are all human.

I - Integrity. These are the values that create the boundaries by which you live that dictate your behavior.

J- Justice. This is the concept of fairness. This is the understanding that to your privilege, you have an obligation to those who have less and those who are vulnerable.

K- Kindness. This is the act of caring for another with no motivational desire to receive anything.

If you combine all of these, it is contained in the next alphabet,

L, which stands for Love. **"**

To respond with compassion in the heat of being triggered comes with practice. If we understand our triggers, if we have prepared for the battle in times of peace, it becomes easy to remember and choose compassion when the going is tough. Regret and happiness are manufactured moment by moment. It only takes a moment of decision, good or bad, to alter the course of our lives.

In the year 218 BC Hannibal, the great Carthaginian strategist and warrior, led his troops from Spain across the Alps against the mighty Rome. His army consisted of more than 38000 soldiers, 8000 horses, and 38 elephants. Hannibal and his troops encountered and overcame extraordinary challenges along the way, crossing the Rhone River and ascending the Alps. However, while trying to come down the mountain, they had to stop because a landslide was blocking a section of the path. Hannibal's army was able to repair the block, but his troops were not convinced that the repaired path could take the weight of all the elephants and horses. Hannibal, who was carrying a walking stick, rammed it into the path to make a point that the ground would hold. It did. But the force of Hannibal ramming his stick into the ground caused an avalanche (perhaps the most devastating avalanche recorded in human history) which killed 18000 of his troops, more than 2000 horses and a good number of elephants. When Hannibal marched to Rome with less than half of his troops and diminished resources, he was defeated by Rome and became a refugee. Hannibal eventually committed suicide by drinking poison. It only took a second of unconsidered action to change the history of the world, as we know it today. It will take only a moment of compassion to change our lives and our world.

Here is an exercise to reflect on your common triggers.

What are some of my common triggers? How do I manage my emotions when I am triggered? How can I respond more compassionately when triggered?

Compassion is a lifesaver

One cannot give compassion without receiving goodness in return. Below is a story whose source I am not sure, but one which moves me deeply.

As part of the holocaust, Nazis would round up Jewish prisoners and transport them to concentration camps, where they would either be sentenced to hard labor or death in the gas chambers. The mode of transportation was cattle trains, which were not meant for human travel. These cattle trains had very little ventilation, no heating, and no toilets. People would be crammed into boxcars, like sardines, for journeys that would sometimes take several days. And sometimes these boxcars would be locked up and abandoned in freezing cold until alternate trains could be found to transport them. Not surprisingly, a significant number of people transported this way died. In one such trip, a boxcar full of Jewish prisoners was abandoned in the middle of winter. As the day progressed into evening and the air became colder and colder, people in that boxcar began to moan and cry. A young girl in the compartment noticed an older woman sitting next to her, shivering uncontrollably. Even though she was cold, the young girl, filled with compassion for the stranger, began rubbing the older lady's back to keep her warm. As the evening progressed into the night, the crying and moaning in the compartment wound down, and by midnight, it became deathly silent. But the young girl continued to rub the older lady's back, giving warmth through a hopeless night. In the morning when soldiers came to open the compartment, only two people were alive- the old lady who had received warmth, and the young girl, who in the process of providing warmth for the other, had inevitably warmed herself.

Compassion saves lives, sometimes in not so dramatic settings as the holocaust. The simple act of noticing suffering and doing something about it can be a life-and-death scenario for someone. **Dr. Kristin Gordon, Educational Consultant; former visiting**

Assistant professor of Sociology at GeorgiaTech shares this experience:

"It was the fifth week of class, and I looked around the room. Trevor (name changed) was missing from class again. He had been missing for several class periods in a row. This was so unlike him. At the beginning of the term, he had been totally engaged. He always came prepared for class and participated in all the activities and discussions. I was getting worried. I told myself, "Well, I'll give it one more class. If he is not here in the next class, I will reach out."

The next class came, and again, Trevor was missing. Ok, it's time to send an email. I knew I had to do something, but I was worried about overstepping the professional boundaries my colleagues and I discussed so frequently. After all, college students are adults, and I was not Trevor's parent. I didn't want to infringe on his privacy or put myself in a place that might compromise my "professional distance" from the students I taught. As I crafted the email, I chose my words carefully. I expressed to Trevor that I was worried about him and his progress in the course. I wanted him to know that I was available to help him catch up with the material and connect him with any additional resources and support he might require.

I anxiously watched for a return email. When it came, I was terrified. Trevor stated that he had not left his room in days. He was struggling and desperately needed help. I did not know what to do. The tone of the email was so full of pain and fear. I didn't know where Trevor was, but I knew someone needed to be with him immediately. I called the dean and asked that someone be sent to his student residence as soon as possible. The dean's office responded quickly, and they found Trevor in his room very much alone and in need of help.

I am a college professor, not a counselor, so I felt fortunate that university resources were in place to take care of Trevor. However, with this particular event, I had a very scary realization. What if I had waited for one more class? What if all of Trevor's professors had waited just a little bit longer? What if we had felt so uncomfortable reaching out to a student on a personal level that no one had responded to Trevor's plea for someone to notice him and help? What if in the name of "professionalism" I had decided that contacting Trevor just wasn't my responsibility, was too personal, would take too much time, or might compromise my success in the classroom? I shudder to think about these "what ifs."

After Trevor began receiving the support and care he required, he came to visit me. I was so grateful to see him. He said something that hit me like the proverbial ton of bricks. He thanked me for reaching out to him and said that I was the first person that had noticed he was missing from classes, meals, activities, everything! I doubt that was the case. I imagine many people noticed that he was missing and worried about him. However, what I fear is that those people, just as I did initially, decided not to take action. They worried and wondered, but they did nothing.

Students live tumultuous lives. Just in the time that I have been teaching, my students have struggled with overt acts of racism on campus (in addition to the constant covert racism many experience every day), sexual assault, mental illness, self-harm, bullying, loss of family members, self-discovery and struggles with personal identity, just to name a few.

There is a great deal of talk about compassion in education. We wouldn't dream of educating our students without a personal connection, right? However, what I have learned from my experience with Trevor and similar experiences with other students, is that feeling empathy for and connection with my students isn't sufficient to be considered compassion. It is not compassion unless one takes action. Sometimes I am aware of the struggles and needs of my students and am able to respond with compassion, and sometimes I miss out on the opportunity to respond. I may perceive myself to be too busy or too tired to take action. Even worse, I may not even notice the pain and struggle of a student right in front of me. Showing compassion is a concern of many teachers. I know I am not alone. I also know that our students need us. They need us to teach them, but they also require us to foster an authentic human connection with them as people. **"**

Work

"Human needs arrange themselves in hierarchies of pre-potency. That is to say, the appearance of one need usually rests on the prior satisfaction of another, more pre-potent need. Man is a perpetually wanting animal. Also, no need or drive can be treated as if it were isolated or discrete; every drive is related to the state of satisfaction or dissatisfaction of other drives." -Maslow, A.H. (1943)[11]

We evolved as hunters.

Our workplace is our new hunting ground. We hunt for financial success, security, and social validation. Our workplaces may be less physically dangerous than the hunting grounds our ancestors faced. But the uncertainties, threats, and competition for survival are no less real for us than they were for our ancestors. The need for social safety, trust, happiness, collegial support, and care is just as, if not more critical, for our excellence now as it was when we were hunters.

Evolutionarily we are designed to perform to our best potential in an environment of trust, safety, happiness, support, and caring. In most organizational settings, these non-tangibles are not even acknowledged. Strangers from diverse backgrounds with diverse viewpoints and personalities suddenly become a part of our 'hunting pack'. Balancing our place in the hunting pack is not easy.

The word work, in itself, can mean different things to different people. Merriam-Webster defines work as 'exerting oneself physically or mentally, especially in a sustained effort for a purpose or under compulsion or necessity.' Unless we are one of those few whose fundamentals of survival- food, shelter, survival, physical safety- are covered by inheritance, we have to seek out professions, earn a living, secure our own needs and the needs of those we love and care for.

For some, work is the very identity of life. For these individuals, everything they think, feel is about work. For others, work is a painfully necessary interruption in the middle of living, which makes survival possible. For some, work is passion; for others, work is a compulsion. For some, work is joy; for others, work is suffering. And these are not permanent identities. Most of us weave between these different emotions through our career and sometimes, even within the course of a single day, we find ourselves vacillating between love and hate for our professions. Challenging times at work are inevitable. While work can be a source of survival and purpose, it can also be a source of suffering. Workplaces are increasingly becoming synonymous with stress, anxiety, and depression. But it doesn't have to be like that.

In 'The Adventures of Tom Sawyer' by Mark Twain, Tom is charged by his aunt to whitewash a 30-yard fence on a Saturday morning. However, Tom does not want to miss out on any of the weekend fun, and more importantly does not want to be ridiculed by the other boys for working on a Saturday. He initially tries to bribe another boy to take his place, but that does not work out. So he changes tactics. When one of the town boys stop to mock him, Tom pretends that he is enjoying his work and claims that it is a privilege to whitewash the fence. This intrigues the boy who trades some of his 'treasures' with Tom for a chance at whitewashing. Soon every boy in town has given up his treasure to Tom for an opportunity to whitewash the fence. Tom's plan is so successful that by mid-afternoon, he not only has completed his 'chore' but also has an array of treasures that have been willingly given to him.

As Mark Twain notes, *"...Work consists of whatever a body is **obliged** to do, and that Play consists of whatever a body is **not obliged** to do...And this would help him to understand why constructing artificial flowers or performing on a treadmill is work, while rolling ten-pins or climbing Mont Blanc is only amusement."*

Life is like a game of Monopoly. The currency is Time. We trade our time to acquire skills. We then trade our time and skills for resources that will meet our needs. Some of our needs are physical, while some are psychological. In 1943, Abraham Maslow published his famous paper on the hierarchy of human needs. His model postulates that the highest human motivation is the search for self-actualization (which is reaching our highest potential).

However, before we do so, our needs for self-esteem must be satisfied. For the self-esteem needs to be addressed, we must feel loved and belonged. Before we are motivated to meet our needs for love and belonging, we must feel safe. But to be motivated to satisfy our safety needs, we must have our basic physiological needs met. His hierarchy of needs diagram illustrates this.

Maslow's hierarchy of needs

We work because we have to or want to. When we work because we have to, work becomes a painful experience. When we work because we want to, work becomes fun and fulfilling. According to the Department of Labor Statistics, we spend 8.5 hours a day on average at work[12]. This comes to 42.5 hours per 5-day workweek. For an average of 47 weeks per year, this amounts to close to 2000 hours every year that we spend at work. Assuming a full 50-year working life, this means close to 100,000 hours of our life spent in the workplace. It would make business sense if, when giving some much of our quality time, we get back not just sustenance for survival, but also happiness, connection, and purpose. If not, we are shortchanging ourselves.

We don't work in a vacuum. We regularly interface with people, with some of us interfacing more than others. The onus is on us to make the time we spend at work happy, meaningful, and fulfilling. While we may not be able to avoid triggers, we can change the lens with which we see and how we interact with the world we live in. We can change the way we influence the world, and if we are in positions of power, we can create the structural framework for compassion, and therefore, happiness and success to unfold.

Suffering and Compassion in the workplace

Suffering happens in the narrow hallways between expectation and reality. It is the sense of unpleasantness and discomfort that arises when our realities do not meet our expectations of harmony. Because our expectations are unique, whether or not situations will cause us suffering is personal. For example, in a 1978 happiness study conducted by Brickman and Coates, the long-term happiness levels of lottery winners and paraplegic victims of severe accidents were studied[13]. Lottery winners took less pleasure than controls in a variety of ordinary events, and in general, were not happier than controls. This is because they were comparing their everyday events to a high point of their life, which was the act of winning the lottery. Victims of accidents were less happy than the controls but had a strong nostalgia for an idealized past. Because they were comparing their present activities to a high point- which was an idealized version of their past, they too were unhappy. Interestingly, the everyday happiness levels of winners and victims were remarkably close. What this study demonstrates is that happiness is relative.

People in resource-poor situations are just as happy as people in resource-rich settings. I have met doctors with 200,000$-plus yearly salaries distressed about how little they were making compared to their peers, and I have met caregivers who make minimum wage expressing how blessed they are compared to some of their peers. As the mindset of entitlement increases in societies, so does its suffering. As John Milton wrote in his book, Paradise Lost, *"The mind is its own place, and in itself can make a heaven of hell, a hell of heaven."*

That said, suffering is unavoidable, including at the workplace. As individuals suffer, the culture of the organization suffers, and as a result, the business outcome of the organization suffers too. This is a two-way process. A suffering organization will, in turn, inflict harm on an otherwise healthy individual. And the challenges become cyclical, and eventually spiral out into the outside environment, creating poor customer service and even companies that create social harm. So when we see an airline that frequently hits the news for how badly it treats its customers or a grocery giant that gains notoriety for poor customer service, it behooves us to dig deeper and ask if this is indicative of human suffering in their workplace.

Here is a smattering of some work behaviors that cause suffering. As you look at the scenarios below, I urge you to ask yourself some difficult questions. You will be revisiting these scenarios once again in the book, after exploring some compassion tools. As you read these scenarios, I invite you to ask yourself some of these questions

Do you know any of these? Are you one of these?

I invite you to lean into each of these situations of suffering below to consider this question: **'What would I do if I were in this situation?'**

Bias:

Adhya comes from a conservative Indian background. She recently started working in a large IT company in San Francisco. She leads a small team of 12 people. One of her team members is Adam. Adam is gay and open about this fact. Adhya, because of her conservative upbringing, sees Adam's sexual preference as morally unacceptable. Even though she is trying to keep her views private, it shows up in how she judges Adam or treats him when things are not going well.

Gossiping at work:

Beatrice recently started working as a teacher's aide in a special needs school. Beatrice is cheerful, talkative, and quickly connects with people. Sharon, another teacher's aide in a different classroom, is going through a difficult relationship with her supervising teacher. She has chosen to keep this to herself for several reasons. One day, when Beatrice and Sharon are alone in the lunchroom, Sharon opens up about her challenges to Beatrice and requests her to keep it secret. Two weeks later, Sharon's supervising teacher confronts Sharon about her talking behind her back. Sharon knows Beatrice must have told others about their private conversation. Sharon is angry and upset that Beatrice broke her trust.

Easily triggered:

Carter is a branch manager for a supermarket chain. He takes his work very seriously. He is very detail-oriented and works very hard to ensure that his branch has no customer complaints. He has a zero-tolerance policy for mistakes by the employees in his branch. Even small infractions are met with very stern warnings. In the past, employees have been fired ungraciously by Carter for workplace errors, or have quit after yelling matches with Carter. No one questions Carter's commitment to the success of his branch, but his brusque personality and unwillingness to provide leeway for even the smallest mistakes make him unpopular. Carter justifies that emotions do not have a role in the workplace.

Entitlement

Dennis, a software engineer, has been in the workforce for about two years. He knows that there is a high demand for talent such as his in Silicon Valley, where he is based. He recently heard that some of his friends in large IT companies get catered meals every day and free cocktails on Friday afternoons. He is otherwise happy with the startup he works for but is upset that he does not get the same kind of perks that his friends at the large IT companies are getting. He is becoming increasingly vocal about these demands.

Incivility

Emelda is a talented Gen-Y employee. Her team meets every week to share progress and set goals. Emelda is always present at these meetings, but when she is not the one presenting, she is always stimming on her phone. Her colleagues find this distracting and somewhat disrespectful. Her boss has discussed this with her, but Emelda justifies that she is indeed listening, and stimming on her phone is not stopping her from paying attention to what is happening in these meetings.

Jealousy

Francis and Mark joined their biotech company as scientists at the same time. At the end of three years, Francis has moved on to become a senior scientist. Mark, who has strong leadership and communication skills, has moved up the ladder quickly to become a project leader- a role that involves supervising a team of senior and junior scientists. Francis is envious of Mark's success. He has not-so-generous interpretations of Mark's success. Francis' envy is affecting his loyalty to his project and his company.

Unfairness

Gordon is a team leader in a retail firm. Among the people, he leads are Carrie and Jenna. Both Carrie and Jenna are hardworking individuals who want to contribute to their work. Carrie is outspoken and does not hesitate to point out mistakes when they happen. She has been in the company longer than Gordon or Jenna. Jenna is more docile and is a people pleaser. Gordon finds it easier to get along with Jenna than with Carrie. When an opening for a senior position in his team opens up, Gordon recommends Jenna for the job, even though Carrie should be the natural choice for the role based on her seniority and her solid track record of success.

Passing blame

Henna is a project manager in an IT consulting company. Her company creates and delivers IT solutions for clients. This is a competitive space, and accuracy is critical for continuing business contracts. Her projects involve a lot of moving parts and rely on clear communication of requirements for success. Her latest project, for a critical client, has failed miserably, causing the client to sign up with a competitor. Henna revisits the stream of communication with her team and realizes that she had overlooked some requirements, which could have caused the failure of the project. However, she knows that she is the only one who will ever know about her oversight, and she could easily save her skin by blaming some of her programmers. Fearful of being reprimanded by her bosses, this is what she chooses to do.

Passive-aggressive behaviors

Ines is a nurse in a city hospital. She is an older person with many years of experience. She does not like Dr. Yin, one of the doctors in her pediatric ward, who she has to work closely with. Yin is a young doctor of Asian origin who is dedicated to her profession as Ines is. Ines is not able to explain why she is biased against Dr. Yin. One day Ines accidentally misplaces a patient file, and Dr. Yin misses the appointment. Dr. Yin confronts Ines about this. Ines is upset but does not want to further the discussion. After this, Ines takes every opportunity to show her disapproval of Dr. Yin. She is looking out for instances where Dr. Yin will make a mistake so that she can be vocal about it. She overdoes her notes- emphasizing that 'some people' will find fault with her if she doesn't. Ines also engages in non-verbal gestures that indicate her displeasure- pouting, frowning, banging notes on the desk- when Dr. Yin is around. Everyone is feeling awkward.

Inconsiderate behaviors

Joubain is a middle-aged employee in a data entry role. He shares a cubicle with two other employees. Joubain owns a pair of cats that he loves very much. He wears clothes to work which have a lot of cat fur on them. Selina, who shares the cubicle with Joubain, is allergic to animal fur. She sneezes and tears up whenever Joubain is near her. She had spoken to Joubain about her allergies and asked him if he would not wear clothes with cat fur to work. Joubain seemed offended by the suggestion and told her that he was not invading her clothes preferences and she should not invade his. With office space being limited, re-situating her desk seems challenging. Selina wishes Joubain would be more considerate of her health.

Manipulative behaviors

Katia is a talented data scientist in a mid-size company. Katia is also very ambitious and believes in 'success-at-any-cost.' She is also very good at hiding her ambition from her peers and projecting a very positive workplace attitude. Her boss, Annabelle, is a kind leader, who wants everyone in her team, including Katia, to succeed. Katia sees an opportunity for progress when Annabelle's new manager, Steve, takes a dislike for Annabelle. Katia secretly colludes with Steve to discredit Annabelle's leadership, with the understanding that she will take on Annabelle's position if she leaves. Thanks to their efforts, Annabelle is removed from her role. Katia has now replaced Annabelle. She starts a covert campaign that she had nothing to do with Annabelle's leaving.

Time wasting behaviors

Li-Xin recently joined a global organization as a staff engineer. Previously, he worked in a demanding, fast-paced startup. He finds work slow and undemanding in his current role. He has realized that there is very little incentive for him to excel and that he can get by as long as he meets basic expectations and maintains good relationships with his peers. While he satisfies the essential office time and output requirements, he is not living to his full potential. Most of his day is spent on discreetly watching movies and playing games on his private laptop in his cubicle.

Nepotism

Maria is the CEO of a mid-sized data analytics company. Her CFO has recently quit, and she wants to fill the role with an internal candidate. Justin and Wendi are both candidates for the role. Justin is several years senior to Wendi and has demonstrated loyalty and excellence in his role. Wendi is also talented and committed. Wendi and Maria belong to the same hometown. Maria is personally fond of Wendi. Maria's bias for working with someone of the same gender and from her hometown ultimately leads her to appoint Wendi as the new CFO. Justin now has to report to a colleague who he once mentored.

Eccentric behaviors

Nathan is a pharmaceutical scientist with sometimes brilliant insights. However, he does not make an effort to document or communicate his ideas. He often blurts out ideas and starts work on new projects without taking the time to discuss them with colleagues and get feedback. Nathan also does not like his proposals being challenged by others. His rather chaotic work style and absence of clear communication have caused challenges in his team. While there has been some success, Nathan's projects have sometimes failed because of his eccentricity. Nathan himself has struggled to put publications together because he had not recorded the data he generated.

Ineffective communication

Olga is a senior director of hardware engineering. She comes from a cultural background where it is acceptable to communicate things as is. Olga has carried her cultural preferences into her job. Even though she means well and she is technically competent, her personality comes across as brusque and abrasive because she tends to state facts without tact. Olga's team members have started complaining to HR about her insensitive emails and conversations. Olga is confused that her good intentions are being misunderstood.

Information hoarding

Patrice is a VP of products in a mid-sized company. Patrice is the link between her company's CXO's and her team. She is very particular about the flow of information across teams and from upper management into hers. She feels it gives her control and power when she can maneuver information. She is fearful that sharing too much information will make her lose her value edge. Her team members, however, feel that Patrice's behaviors signals distrust, and insist on the need to be in the loop with relevant information. Other teams feel that her disinclination to share information stumps collaborative opportunities. Patrice justifies to herself that she be perceived this way rather than be taken advantage of.

Laziness/Procrastination

Quentin is a recent college grad who has started work as a floor employee in a large grocery store. Quentin is not inspired to work or driven to succeed. The only reason he comes to work is for the money. He uses every opportunity he gets to escape to the break room, where he spends time on social media. Quentin does not seem very bothered when his supervisors are upset with him. He feels there will always be opportunities for low paying jobs like his.

Team Mismatch

Robert is a young engineering graduate with grand ideas. He is full of enthusiasm and driven to create and test new projects. Robert recently joined an engineering team in a famous company. The team he has joined is mostly made of older peers with much less enthusiasm for implementing new ideas. Most suggestions that Robert makes are turned down with a terse, 'We don't do things that way around here.' Robert feels frustrated, but working for a big company as a fresh graduate is appealing to him.

Bullying/Abuse

Stephen is a chief medical officer in a biotech firm. He can be very charming to some and very acrid to others, depending on the situation. Among the people he supervises is James, a mild-mannered scientist who is very intelligent, but does not communicate well. Stephen instinctively realizes that James is an easy target. Stephen starts insulting James in private and in group meetings- often disguising his insults as jokes. James does not know how to respond to Stephen's onslaughts and chooses to keep silent. Stephen, seeing a lack of resistance from James, steps up his attacks. With time, Stephen assails James' contribution, ethics, and even his appearance. In a recent group meeting, Stephen yelled at James' perceived incompetence and called him an uncomplimentary name. James is upset, angry, and confused.

Misplaced personal boundaries

Tina, a boisterous middle-aged woman, comes from deeply religious culture. She works as a nursing aide in a big city hospital system. Her coworker Alexa is an atheist. She is a quiet woman who has recently gone through a slew of unfortunate personal experiences. Tina is convinced that Alexa's suffering stems from a lack of religious faith. She firmly believes that if Alexa were to turn to her faith, she would find true solace. Tina has started hounding Alexa with invitations to attend her church and explore her faith. Alexa appreciates Tina's concern but is flustered that her tragedies are being linked to her personal faith. She feels Tina is adding to existing stress.

Conflict makers

Uma is a teacher in an elementary school. She is sometimes inappropriately curious about the people around her. Also, when she gathers information, she tends to pass it on for maximal sensational impact. Ryan and Sally, her coworkers, recently had a misunderstanding. They have both said uncomplimentary things about each other in private, which Uma is privy to. Uma rallies these conversations to Ryan and Sally, causing an escalation of the issue. This results in a full-blown conflict between Ryan and Sally.

Emotionally unstable behaviors

Vanessa supervises a fulfillment facility for a large online retailer. Most of her staff are seasonal employees who are unskilled and work at near minimum-wage salaries. Vanessa is known to be unpredictable in her behavior towards her team. On some days, she is kind and considerate, and on others, she is belligerent and abusive. Sometimes she throws public tantrums and insults employees for minor infractions. Her wavering personality makes her a challenging person to work with. Her company leadership does not seem to care as she is consistently able to meet their business expectations. Some people have quit, and those who have chosen to stay are feeling fearful and helpless.

Credit stealers

Walter leads a small team of chemists in a chemical company developing polymers. Among the people reporting to Walter is a passionate young chemist, Penelope. Penelope, through personal initiative, hard work, and perseverance has discovered an innovative process that can save the company a lot of time and money. Penelope presents the discovery to Walter. Walter is full of praise for Penelope privately. In the next meeting for executives, in which Penelope is not present, Walter carefully words the presentation such that it appears that the idea is his own and Penelope as merely the person who did the work. Walter is praised by his management and promised a bonus. Penelope's single-handed contribution to the project is now diluted, as she is seen as merely a hand in the discovery.

Takers

Xavier is a programmer in a software company. He has his feelers out for opportunities that will further his growth. Xavier is quick to ask for favors and does not voluntarily reciprocate. He receives willingly but thinks hard before giving anything. If anyone does not give what he asks for, he is quick to condone them for their stinginess. Over time, people have come to avoid his company, knowing that he will not hesitate to take advantage of their generosity.

Impossible expectations

Yasmin is a project manager at an outsourcing company. Her role is to ensure the quality and timeliness of deliverables. Her latest project for a high profile global client will, contingent upon its success, likely set her up for promotion. Wanting to create a positive impression about her leadership, Yasmin promises an unreasonable timeline for completion. She then proceeds to transfer the pressure of the impossible deadline on her team. Yasmin is willing to sacrifice her team's work-life balance, and likely lead them to burnout for a personal stake.

Non-appreciators

When Zara joined the customer experience team, she was given a grand vision of how her role would influence the success of their products. Inspired, Zara gave the project all she could, often going beyond the call of duty to ensure customer satisfaction. Come bonus time, after nearly a year of late nights and weekend work; she expects that her contributions would earn her due reward. However, to her disappointment, she receives no commendation for her efforts. Zara's boss tells her, it would be unfair for her colleagues if only she gets a bonus. Zara is disappointed. She sees no reason why she would work any harder than the others going forward.

As we encounter challenges like these, we are left to wonder what our course of action should be. Most of us like to see, not just the situation, but the root of the challenges addressed. We want to see happiness and fairness. We want to see win-wins. However, many traditional responses leave people feeling slighted, ignored, helpless, and angry. Many of these are cookie-cutter solutions to unique problems. They do not work.

And here is proof:

- 70% of employees are disengaged, causing losses of $500 Billion/year- Gallup[14]

- 40% of employees leave their jobs because they are unhappy with it- IBM[15]

- 75% of the workplace says that their bad boss is the worst part of their workplace- Gallup[16]

- 83% of employees are stressed at work. The annual cost of stress is estimated at $300 Billion/year- Everest[17]

- The probability of job turnover in companies with weak company cultures is 70%- Columbia College[18]

These data are only the tip of the iceberg. When a company's efforts to reduce any of these symptoms of workplace suffering are not paired with the internal transformation of individuals, it is met with derision. As individuals shift, so does the fabric of the system. What is needed is a set of tools that allow individuals to become the answers to their workplace problems. I propose that the practice of compassion is the most meaningful and effective approach to address workplace challenges.

> "Compassion belongs to every sphere of activity, including, of course, the workplace."
> — His Holiness the Dalai Lama

Compassion is the most effective framework for addressing workplace suffering because it changes the very construct of the individuals who make the organization. As many drops of water make the mighty ocean, so is a compassionate organization built of many compassionate individuals. Because compassionate organizations are founded on human motivation, they are powerful and resilient in the face of challenges. A culture of compassion can be HR's greatest friend in preventing negative instances and in resolving conflict. Compassion tends to be mirrored. If one sees a compassionate act in the workplace, they likely feel motivated to be compassionate to someone else they encounter. Compassion can ripple out into the world, to 3 degrees of separation.

One of the common misconceptions about compassion is that it a soft skill that is not business relevant. Nothing can be farther from the truth. As we discussed above, workplaces can have a lot of suffering- stress, anxiety, personality conflicts, misplaced expectations, timelines, gossip, unfairness, bias, bullying, and more. People deal with it by trying to isolate work from 'life'. Compartmentalization of work and life is not always possible or sustainable. There are always bound to be carryovers. The solution is not sweeping workplace suffering under the rug, but addressing the suffering by training for and reinforcing compassion as a cultural tenet of the organization. Compassion makes business sense. As we will see in the following pages, compassion improves innovation, improves loyalty, reduces stress and anxiety, decreases absenteeism, and creates a happier, low-conflict work environment. Organizations spend enormous amounts of resources in trying to improve health and happiness. Compassion skills can make all these needs happen in a human-centric, cost-effective way.

Workplace Compassion

IS NOT/DOES NOT	IS/DOES
Weakness	Power
Religious practice	Spiritual growth
Compromise business success	Empowers business success
Not work relevant	Very work relevant
Not teachable/learnable	Can be learnt/taught
Involves large resources	Involves intention and action
Solely for leadership	Involves all in the organization

When workplaces are compassionate, they thrive. People are motivated to give because that is where their purpose lies. This is not a lofty thought. There is accumulating proof to demonstrate the business value of compassion.

- For example, the top ten performing companies in the "Global Empathy Index" generated 50% more net income per employee than the bottom ten companies[19].

– 70% of people in an NBC survey said they would forego a 10% raise for a kinder boss[20].

– Workplace happiness, which is a direct outcome of a compassionate culture, also impacts business success. Companies with happy employees outperform their competition by 20%[21].

– Productivity improves by 20-25% in organizations with connected employees, which, again, is facilitated by compassionate behaviors[22].

Here is a real-life example of workplace compassion in action. This story illustrates how compassion can create loyalty in organizations.

Dr. Kannan (Name changed)
Scientist, Napoli, Italy

"I was 35, and I was dying.

I was a cell biologist studying intracellular membrane traffic in Napoli, Italy. I had come here for my post-doctoral studies many years before and had stayed on to pursue a career in science. Napoli is generally a very kind place. People here seem to care for others naturally. Even though I am an immigrant here, my lab and my research institute have treated me as one of their own.

It started with pain in my abdomen, but with time, the pain became intolerable. There came the day when I had to be rushed to the ER. A slew of tests could not place the cause of my pain. My abdomen meanwhile continued to bloat, and I became a human pincushion as the doctors frantically poked and biopsied me. Even though they never told me directly, my multiple visits to the cancer ward told me that they suspected cancer. I was right. About a month after my admission into the hospital, the verdict finally came: I had advanced cancer of the stomach. I was given two weeks to live.

With my own family 4000 miles in my hometown in India, my colleagues became my family. Through the entire ordeal, my supervisor and my colleagues were my constant source of support and comfort. They made sure that not a day went by when I was alone in the hospital. There was always someone from my lab by my bedside, at lunch and evening visiting hours, every single day I was in the hospital. The hospital food was crappy, so my colleagues made sure to bring fresh home-cooked meals every day. One of the people who supported me tremendously was my supervisor's wife. She took on a motherly role, even offering to wash and fold my clothes at her home, as I lay helplessly in the hospital. I was overwhelmed by the generosity and compassion that my colleagues were unconditionally giving me.

This painful time was also a time for potent wisdom for me. I lay in my bed, a human pincushion, thinking about the things that mattered in my life. I realized that knowledge, fame, and money meant little in the face of looming death. Only one thing seemed important to me at that time- I wanted to taste my mother's lentil soup. I had grown up eating it and had never really appreciated it, but at this time, it was the only thing that seemed relevant. My brush with death was also my call to gratitude.

Scientists like to question data. My friends and colleagues, trained as scientists, realized that there could be alternate explanations to the data that was coming from my diagnostic tests. They roped in other experts for opinion, including a colleague's family member who was the head of the diagnostic lab in a nearby hospital. So, more tests, more results. I remember the day the final verdict came. I was in bed, two other patients in my room, when the head of the hospital bursts in, all excited, screaming, "You have Tuberculosis!" It turned out that I had tuberculosis in my stomach, and the disease had lingered long enough to create cancer-like symptoms. It was curable. I was going to live after all!

When my colleagues at the research center heard about this, they turned out en masse into the hallways screaming, "Kannan has tuberculosis." There was so much celebration for my tuberculosis that the director of the institute had to come and quiet them down. I never thought that anyone's tuberculosis diagnosis could be celebrated with so much glee!

Two weeks later, I walked out of the hospital that I thought I was never going to leave alive.

I am forever thankful for the lessons in gratitude that my experience of dying brought for me. It is truly a blessing to have kind colleagues who care for you when you are down. My brush with death made me realize what it means to work in a compassionate workplace, and why I would never work in any other place but this one. **"**

And it is not just in the safe sanitized settings of the lab that compassion shows up. Compassion shows us even in the tough engagement of the armed forces. **Adam Burn** is a **US Air Force veteran** and currently a **Teacher of compassion**.

"I believe compassion to be a core motivation for serving in the military, " he shares. "Compassion showed up in simple ways, like when we ran low on food and shared our limited supply with each other, even though we were hungry ourselves. It showed up when we listened to each other while overseas over what we missed about home and the people we left behind. It showed up when we told a buddy we'd cover his shift so he could be with his wife and kids for a birthday. There may not be the exultation of compassion in its purest emotional expression as other circles may prefer, but that doesn't mean it doesn't show up in military contexts. Sometimes it is the subtler expressions of compassion that were just enough to get us through the tough days, if by any means, than simply the knowledge that we were not there alone. **"**

Accepting Compassion

Receiving compassion is as critical a skill as giving compassion.

When we see the world with paranoia, every interaction is laced with ulterior motives. It blocks us from accepting that the people who are kind to us are authentic and have noble intent. The opposite of paranoia is pronoia, which as writer Perry Barlow pointed out is *'the suspicion that the universe is conspiring on your behalf.'* That openness for receiving compassion, a sort of practical pronoia, is essential for compassion to be sustainable. Opening up to compassion may require us to become vulnerable, but that is how compassion unfolds.

Karen Palmer, Founder of GlobalKindness Going Viral, shares how her act of opening up herself to the compassion of strangers moved her from homelessness to abundance.

"I have been working for years as a conscious dog trainer and environmental education. I had always felt a deep connection with animals and nature. It was easy for me to see the oneness in animals and nature. With humans, that was a different story. I am a survivor of domestic abuse, and for many years, I suffered in silence and became homeless. I had lost all faith in humans and had many trust issues, but I really wanted a friend, so I decided to adopt a puppy. Little did I know that puppy would change my life. This beautiful puppy I named Lucky, and she lived up to her name on so many occasions. She was pure unconditional love, and she looked at me that way. Soon I was learning to love myself the way my puppy loved me. She had this gift of connection, and when people visited, she was so loving and trusting. It made me want to trust again too.

I remember reading a book, 'You'll see it when you believe it' by Dr. Wayne Dyer and in this book was a quote that really amazed me. It was by Albert Einstein. It stated, "The most important question you can ask yourself is, do I live in a friendly or hostile universe?" That quote stopped me in my tracks. I took a deep breath and looked very closely at how I saw the world. I asked myself what I believed. At that point, I had been learning the Universal Laws, which states we attract what our most dominant beliefs are. I realized my most dominant belief at that time in my life was I deserve this treatment. I still remember looking at my Lucky Girl as I reread those words. Unlike me, she saw our world as a friendly place. I thought to myself could I do that too, maybe just as a science experiment I would give it a shot. I decided to open myself up to compassion. In that instant things changed and miracles began to happen. Strangers came and brought my dog food and me. People invited me to use their shower, and a wonderful couple that owned a restaurant offered me a job and said I could bring my puppy to stay on the patio while I worked. It was because of the kindness of strangers that I got off the streets and Lucky and I were no longer homeless. That was when I realized that the universe is naturally compassionate, but I was the one who had the keys to the doors to let the compassion in. The kindness and compassion of those strangers showed me changed my life forever. I am now a Global Kindness Leader and Educator; I get to help people; I am a best-selling author and popular online talk show host. I focus on the kindness and compassion in our world. I see the oneness in people, pets, and our planet. I understand we are all connected, and this has made my life a dream come true. I am grateful I can help others to remember their magnificence and see the oneness. My new most dominant belief is I deserve a beautiful life, we all do. **"**

Stepping into action

It is easy being a couch critic. Many of us feel like we have paid our dues once we have made our comments and offered criticism in a social forum. This is perhaps one of the greatest challenges facing our society today. We stroll from issue to issue, passing judgments, and feeling smug that we have made a difference. The more vocal we are, the more aggressive the language of our criticism is, the more we feel like activists. Our criticism, often instead of helping the situation, discourages and hurts people on the field who are doing real work. Let me illustrate.

One of the most poignant images of the 20th century is a photograph of the famine in Sudan from 1993. It shows a child fallen to the ground, crawling toward a United Nations food camp a kilometer away. A vulture is waiting for him to die so he can eat him. The photographer, a young man named Kevin Carter, won the Pulitzer Prize for photography for this photograph. His photograph created a global response and helped alleviate the situation in Sudan. But Carter himself became the victim of great hate, some calling him a vulture for taking the picture but not rescuing the child, which was true. Soon after Carter took the picture, he boarded a flight and left the place, after shooing away the vulture. But this seemingly callous act of Carter was prefaced by a lifetime of witnessing and capturing images in some of the most painful human conflicts. His portfolio of images- including those of shootings, beheadings, and people being burnt to death alive with tires filled with gasoline around their necks- required that he practice emotional detachment from the horror he was highlighting to the world. While his critics were tucked into the comfort of their personal lives, Carter was trying to stay sane amidst the blood and gore he was witnessing every day. After his Pulitzer Prize, Carter simply could not handle the mounting criticism. Broken by the horror of the pain he had witnessed and the hate that was piling up, he committed suicide in early 1994 by carbon monoxide poisoning.

Carter's diary shows that the situation had indeed moved him. "I see all this, and all I can think of is Megan (his young daughter)". He told his friend at the site, and later wrote this in his diary: "Dear God, I promise I will never waste my food no matter how bad it can taste and how full I may be, I pray that He will protect this little boy, guide and deliver him away from his misery. I pray that we will be more sensitive towards the world around us and not be blinded by our own selfish nature and interests." While Carter's life was cut short, the little boy in his photograph survived. The boy grew up into adulthood and died in 2007 due to health challenges.

Do you think the critics who were so vocal about Carter's morality, took ownership for their role in his suicide? I believe not. I believe not many even noticed. The responsibility for his death was likely distributed to the collective commons, and people quickly turned on to someone else to criticize.

This is not a standout example. Every single day, media feed us increasingly sensational news to stir up an increasingly numbing brain. Our natural instinct is to step into action to relieve the suffering, but feel helpless by the magnitude of the issue. Therefore, we do that 'little-bit' to add to the relief efforts by adding our voices to it. However, unless our voices are voices of help (for example, signing a change.org petition), they are better not added to the pool.

And no, we cannot be the solution to every problem out there. Compassion is noticing, feeling, and non-judgmental action for the suffering we encounter. Self-compassion is knowing and accepting our personal limitations and being able to do so without guilt. Wisdom, in this case, is learning to walk the middle path between action and inaction. We can be the change we want to see in the world.

The measure of our divinity is how much better we have left our world compared to how we found it.

Before we end this chapter let us spend a moment on self-reflection.

What opportunities do I see for practicing compassion in my day-to-day living in my personal life?

_____

_____

_____

_____

_____

_____

_____

_____

_____

_____

_____

_____

_____

_____

_____

_____

_____

What opportunities do I see for practicing compassion in my day-to-day living in my professional life?

_____

_____

_____

_____

_____

_____

_____

_____

_____

_____

_____

_____

_____

_____

_____

_____

_____

_____

_____

SECTION 2:
THE 9-PILLARS OF WORKPLACE COMPASSION

Some Pies Are Made of
Creamy Velvety Blue
Goodness

Introduction to the 9-Pillars

Now that we have discussed the why, what, when, and where of workplace compassion, the next step is to understand the how.

In this section, we will explore a compassion training framework- the 9-Pillars- that can give you the necessary tools and skills to respond compassionately in the presence of, or absence of triggers. The 9-Pillars are life values we grew up with, but which we often forget in the hustle of survival. When applied appropriately, these 9-Pillars will create a response to challenges that are both compassionate and wise.

This section offers an exploration of these nine values in the context of the workplace, in a very pragmatic way. I have been teaching these 9-Pillars in various settings now- to big teams and small offices, from software firms to dental offices, and to individuals who I have coached. The impact has been universally phenomenal. This is because these 9-Pillars are part of our fundamental thinking and being and easy to resonate with. However, making the 9-Pillars as the true north of our living will require us to shift from inside. The change that we wish to see manifest in the world has to start from within us. So my invitation to you, as you explore the next several pages is to approach the ideas within with openness and authenticity.

Imagine each of these 9-Pillars as power tools that you will hang in your tool belt. When you have experimented and adopted these 9-Pillars, you will know to reach down to your tool belt and know which one to pick to address the task at hand. When you have done this multiple times, your compassion responses will become quicker and more effective. You will experience more peace, happiness, and win-wins the more you play around with these 9-pillars. Discussions of each of these chapters are designed, to be honest, and interactive. The more you experiment, the more you will gain.

Without any more ado, here are the nine pillars of workplace compassion:

1. **Self-compassion:** The ability to be good friends to ourselves
2. **People first thinking:** Prioritizing people and making them feel valued
3. **Abundance mindset:** Seeing and being abundant with life
4. **Mindfulness:** Creating the space between stimulus and response
5. **Embracing Oneness:** Embracing the fact that we are a shared humanity
6. **Communication:** Effectively expressing compassion
7. **Vulnerability:** Being courageous to be appropriately authentic
8. **Big picture thinking:** Approaching life with perspective and purpose
9. **Gratitude:** Knowing that everything that we are and have is a blessing

It may not be easy to remember these 9-pillars in a jiffy. Which is why I created the mnemonic you saw at the beginning of this chapter. I love the blueberry pies my daughter bakes, so this is an easy mnemonic for me.

Some Pies Are Made Of Creamy Velvety Blue Goodness

In the tradition of neuro-linguistic programming, I have created a happy spot in my mind about slices of pie that are covered with a good slathering of velvety blue cream. This image is my anchor to remember the 9-compassion tools in my tool belt. If you choose to come up with your own mnemonic for these 9-pillars that is awesome too!

Here is another important thing:

To access your personal compassion tool kit in times of suffering, you must first remember that there is a toolkit waiting for you to use. There is the primary layer of conditioning that needs to happen to shift to compassion mode. This is what you can do:

In every interaction and every possible opportunity, remind yourself that there is a compassion choice. I do this by asking this simple question:

'What is the most compassionate thing I can do in my current situation?'

Asking this question repeatedly in situations makes compassion our knee-jerk response, like getting into a car and driving for the thousandth time. The brain automatically will search for answers- and the answers happen to be in our tool belts, at arm's length.

Onward to the 9-Pillars of workplace compassion!

Self-Compassion?

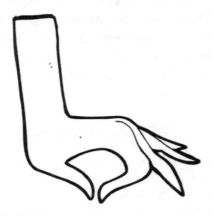

What is Self-Compassion?

Pioneering self-compassion researcher, author, and teacher, Dr. Kristen Neff describes self-compassion as *treating yourself as you would treat a good friend*[1]. As with the definition of compassion, self-compassion involves noticing personal suffering, feeling for our pain, suspending judgments, and stepping into action to alleviate the suffering.

Self-compassion is the foundation on which all other compassion practices are built. We cannot give what we do not have. This is true of compassion as well. Oxygen masks drop down in airplanes when air pressure comes down. Unless we use the oxygen masks ourselves first, we will not be in a position to help a neighbor with theirs. When our brain is deprived of oxygen, our ability to make appropriate choices comes down dramatically. When we cannot show compassion for ourselves, our capacity to show compassion for others comes down significantly. When we deny ourselves the life-saving oxygen that compassion is for our mind and soul, we choke our ability to show up as the best versions of ourselves at work, home, and elsewhere.

Dr. Neff describes self-compassion as being "kind and understanding when confronted with personal failings[2]". According to Dr. Neff, there are three elements to self-compassion.

- Being kind toward oneself without judgment
- Accepting that personal suffering and inadequacies are part of common humanity
- To find mindful balance without getting swept into the negativity of situations

Why Self-Compassion?

Self-compassion is a reference frame with which we experience the world. When we give ourselves kindness, the world we interface with seems kinder. When we give ourselves the benefit of the doubt, we are able to assume noble intent in other's actions. When we are not too hard on ourselves, we are allowing for healing to happen. Self-compassion is a journey to inner harmony. To practice self-compassion, we need to confront our limiting perspectives and fears. We need to address the blocks that come in the way of our being compassionate to ourselves- guilt, anger, resentment, and self-doubt. We emerge not only as kinder people, but also more resilient and influential.

In the workplace, it is becoming increasingly important to practice self-compassion. Grueling demands from work blur the line between life at work and life outside work. Self-compassion can be a check-and-balance skill that allows us to say no to demands that are not meaningful for us in the long run, and make those pivotal decisions with courage.

Self-compassion, as a compassion pillar, can be the wisdom component of compassion. I used to be one of those people who could not say no without feeling very guilty. When anyone came to me with requests for my time or resources, I felt obliged to give. Then one of my mentors showed me that much of my giving was from a place of fear and imbalance. When I said yes, I was often doing it begrudgingly, and I was taking time and resources away from my family. I have learned since that I am not the solution for every challenge in the world, but I will do what I can when I can, with compassion, without compromising on what is important for me. Self-compassion has helped me set boundaries and helped me avoid burnout.

The question I ask myself now is this, 'What is the most compassionate response from me in the face of suffering, *which is also self-compassionate?*'

I use this Zen story as an example :

A Zen master was about to walk into a forest when people from a nearby village stopped him. They warned him about a dangerous snake that lived in the forest. The snake was scaring and biting the villagers who dared entered his domain. Unfazed, the Zen master walked into the woods, where sure enough, the snake came rushing toward him. But the Zen master was not afraid. The snake was surprised by the master's fearlessness. The master and the snake had a conversation in which the master showed the snake the error of his ways. At the end of the conversation, the snake promised the master that he would no longer hurt anyone and that he would practice compassion for all, going forward.

Three months later, the master passed by the same forest, and he saw the snake on the forest floor, all bloodied up and about to die. The shocked master gently picked up the snake and asked him what had happened.

"Once the villagers found that I was not going to hurt them, they started chasing me. The children started throwing rocks at me. Yesterday a group of the villagers beat me up with sticks and left me for dead."

"Why did you not fight back? Why did you not bite them when they attacked you?" asked the master.

"I wanted to. But I promised you that I was going to show compassion for everyone. So I could not hurt them." whispered the snake.

"Yes," replied the master with great sorrow, "but, why did the thought of compassion for everyone exclude you? Did you not realize that your first act of compassion was to protect yourself?

Blocks to self-compassion

Here is a simple truth. Be kind to your body, and your body will be kind to you. Be kind to your mind, and your mind will be kind to you.

As intuitive as self-compassion sounds and feels, this is something we often forget to give to ourselves. Several mental blocks stop us from giving the tenderness and love that we deserve. One apparent block is a lack of acknowledgment that we need self-compassion. Fear of being kind to self and a lack of skills add to the self-compassion lack. Dealing with blocks and working on building self-compassion skills becomes even more difficult when the right work culture is missing. A common objection I see to self-compassion is this: *"In my current phase in life, I cannot afford to prioritize me. Taking time for myself is taking away time from my family and work."* The reality is, self-compassion is no less essential for our wellbeing than sleeping or eating. We can indeed save time by not eating or sleeping, but we will burn out and crash very quickly.

The image below lists some of the common objections, fears and misconceptions around self-compassion. In the following pages, we will look at some of these blocks in more detail.

Blocks to Self Compassion

LIMITING PERCEPTIONS

 Confusing self-compassion with self-pity, selfishness and self-indulgence

 Associating self-esteem with perfection. Not realizing that perfection is a moving target.

 Illusion of strength. Lack of awareness and acknowledgement of personal suffering.

 Confusing personal suffering with personal failings and creating guilt cycles.

FEAR AND CONDITIONING

 Fear of 'looking-inward' and therefore missing out on real healing. Patching up pain with unsustainable 'band-aid' solutions.

 Conditioned fear of gentleness toward self (the idea that we need to be hard on ourselves to feel worthy).

 Fear that if we give ourselves slack, we will derail from our success track. Fear of being left out.

 Inability to let-go and forgive.

 Gremlin voices that reinforce the 'I am not good enough' belief.

CULTURAL SETTINGS

 Social permissions to be kind to oneself

Self-Pity, Self-Indulgence, Selfishness, and Self-Compassion

Confusing these 'Self-' terms creates a lot of confusion, simply because there is so much mental narrative that we carry about these terms. Here is a simple way to differentiate between these terms. Self-compassion is empowering. Self-pity, Selfishness, and Self-indulgence are all disempowering, and very often self-destructive. Self-compassion, on the other hand, is all about balance. Self-compassion is rooted in awareness and foresight.

This image below highlights some of the thought processes between self-compassion and her lesser cousins.

Acknowledging Personal suffering

We are human. We fail; we suffer. When we fail to acknowledge the presence of suffering or interpret suffering as a reflection of personal failing - we become discompassionate to our own selves. Many alpha leaders have grown up with the notion that to lead, one has to simply grit their teeth and push forward through suffering. This is a dialog that is often reinforced by popular cultural narratives. But life is both hard and tender moments in good measure. If we fail to look inward and live out our tender moments, we are not leading a fulfilling life. Telling ourselves that we do not need compassion because we are strong, is saying that we do not need oxygen, because oxygen is for the weak. The more compassionate we become toward ourselves, the stronger we are able to interface with the outside world.

It takes vulnerability to acknowledge personal suffering. But unless we open our hearts to our suffering, unless we become aware of the ways suffering shows up in our lives and how we deny it its rightful identity, we will not have opportunities to address it.

And even as we acknowledge suffering, it is crucial to step away from the judgment that comes with it. A non-self-compassionate thought could be 'I suffer. I am a failure. I deserve this suffering'. A self-compassionate view, on the other hand, could be 'Suffering is unavoidable and universal. What can I do about mine?'

What areas of suffering in my life should I acknowledge to help me become more compassionate toward myself?

_____

_____

_____

_____

_____

_____

_____

_____

_____

_____

_____

_____

_____

_____

_____

_____

_____

_____

_____

SELF-CRITICISM

We do not realize how much criticism we ply on ourselves until we deliberately look at how we go about our lives. I had a coach who suggested I journal my self-criticisms over three days. So for three days, I carried a little journal with me, making short notes whenever I caught myself being self-critical. I ended up with five pages of notes at the end of three days. When I took this over to my coach, he said, "If you were to be as critical of a friend as you are to yourself, I guarantee that your friendship is a lost cause."

Here is a little personal exercise to try out.

Gift yourself a criticism free day (CFD). Make a commitment that anything you do on CFD, you will see in the kindest light possible. If criticisms show up, remember that today is CFD and criticisms will have to wait. Avoid the temptation to overthink.

At the end of your CFD

- **How did you feel?**
- **What shifted?**
- **Why can't every day be a CFD?**

_____

_____

_____

_____

_____

_____

_____

_____

_____

_____

_____

_____

_____

_____

_____

_____

_____

_____

_____

The perfection impasse

One of the common excuses for self-criticism is the pursuit of perfection. But, what was perfect yesterday is far from perfect today. Sometimes the desire to be perfect becomes a self-defeating tool. Perfectionists seed their own failure because their imaginary standards will not let them put out into the world their 'less-than-perfect' creations. Not to mention that the striving for self-perfection causes mental angst and stagnation.

This is not to challenge the striving for excellence or the desire to give our very best. The pursuit of excellence is real; the pursuit of perfection is a fool's errand.

When you feel compelled to pursue perfection at the cost of self-compassion, try replacing it with **Kaizen**. Kaizen is a Japanese term for continuous improvement. The goal is to be a little better today than you were yesterday. A popular suggestion for Kaizen is to strive to increase everyday progress by a 1% margin and let the power of accumulation work its magic. Here is a small exercise to get past the perfection impasse and kick-start kaizen in your life.

What are three areas of my life where a need for perfection is hurting compassion for myself? What opportunities do I see for applying the Kaizen principle of continuous improvement in these areas?

_____

_____

_____

_____

_____

_____

_____

_____

_____

_____

_____

_____

FEAR AND CONDITIONING

One of the great misconceptions we carry is that we have to be hard on ourselves to feel worthy. Self-worth and self-compassion are not inversely proportional. They are, in fact, directly correlated. The more we treat ourselves with kindness, the more worthy we feel. Unfortunately, most of us have grown up in a world where we believe that we are always being judged and unless we push ourselves really hard to meet the needs of those imaginary expectations, we are losers. This is a concept that has been taught to us right from childhood, where we have been graded for relative performance and punished for not meeting them. I believe it is time for us to free ourselves from those limiting fears. The story below illustrates how it took a successful professional some painful life experiences to discover self-compassion.

Dan Waldschmidt
Business Strategist and Author, 10th person on the planet to Run Everest

"One of the greatest superpowers we have in business is this idea of having a chip on your shoulder. It's this idea that you have something to prove- you are going to find a way to be successful despite all the craziness that's in your way. When anyone told me I couldn't do something growing up, I was immediately on a mission to prove them wrong. In my twenties, I achieved some pretty incredible things businesswise. But, what is useful can become a burden. In my case, the chip on my shoulder, which drove me to business success, created collateral damage to my health and relationships.

When you go many sleepless nights, you tear apart your immune system. This is not something you can undo with a snap of your fingers. The last six months before I sold my company, I was so fatigued. Two or three different occasions, I even fell and passed out. I concussed my head against the floor just because of how tired I was.

One of the areas I saw immediate impact was on my personal relationships, with my wife, my kids, and those around me. What's hard is that the people you expect should forgive you for your actions are the people you have hurt the most with your oversight. It's not easy to rebuild those relationships. I would get so frustrated that I could not get these people to forgive me and give me a fresh slate to move on.

In those times of frustration, I would put on my running shoes and run. Sometimes I would run for 2 or 3 hours straight. I did this because running gave me a chance to clear my thoughts. It gave me a certain solace. And while running, you watch yourself behave. First, you are frustrated, angry, and you use all of your rage on running. And when you reach your limit- because you have run out of carbohydrates and hydration- your body kicks in and says you should stop. When you are a novice, you tend to ignore the signs. This is when you could cause yourself significant injury or even die. Running, and observing myself while running, taught me why self-compassion was essential.

Self-compassion teaches us to take care of ourselves. Self-compassion at first glance might seem soft, less machismo that what is needed to succeed in the dog eat dog business world. Part of self-compassion is knowing not just what you can do, but what you should do. Often we don't self-reflect because we are driven to prove someone wrong. *Life is not a sprint; it is a marathon.* Self-compassion teaches us to take care of ourselves. It also helps to remember that just because something is fun does not mean we are not working hard enough. If I were to use the same mindset for competition today as I had then, I could never win a race, much less finish a race.

In those early days, when I was not taking care of myself. I was angry with myself and others. I acted badly. But when I slowed down to re-energize, I was able to say, 'Wait a minute, We are all flawed. This body is the container for me as long as I am here. And if I show a bit of compassion for myself first, I equip myself not just to finish the journey, but to do it at a high level." I now know that when I make time for physical and emotional needs, it doesn't mean that I am weak, it doesn't mean I am distracted. It just means I am recognizing that the journey of life is a long one, and with self-compassion, I am preparing myself for success. **"**

Dan's experience is a reminder to slow down for self-introspection and self-care in the bustle of work. Here are some **self-compassion affirmations** that you can reflect on and make as your own:

"I do not have to bully myself into feeling worthy. I can give myself all the self-compassion need. My compassion for myself will not make me weak. It will make me stronger, resilient, and more authentic. I do not need to meet some imaginary standard of excellence to feel worthy. There is only one standard for excellence. Me. If I am a little better today than yesterday, I am on the excellence track. Being kind to myself will in no way hurt my progress as a leader, as a colleague, and as a human being."

GREMLINS

Another major childhood conditioning that blocks self-compassion are 'the gremlin voices' in our heads. I want to spend some time discussing gremlins since this is one of the most potent psychological blocks to self-compassion.

Gremlins are inner-critics; the incessant voice in your head that says,

' I am not good enough because...; I cannot allow myself to shine because...; I do not deserve this because... '

Every step of your life marathon, your gremlin throws a block.

In the early days of the aircraft industry, Gremlins was a slang used to indicate mischievous folkloric creatures that hid in airplanes and would cause aircraft malfunction by cutting critical wires with their sharp teeth. The lore of gremlins carried over into literature. Roald Dahl wrote a book about gremlins, Walt Disney used them in cartoons, movies were made, and the idea of Gremlins was adapted into coaching parlance as well.

Gremlins are very difficult to work with because they camouflage themselves as voices of reason and self-preservation. It is true that at some point in our lives, Gremlins hatched to protect us from harm and shame. But they stick around long after their role is complete. This is where they become harmful rather than helpful.

Let's take the case of Anne, a fourth-grader who is giving a talk in her school assembly.

Halfway through her talk, she blanks out. She looks at the assembly and her teachers. Everyone is looking at her. Anne is scared and ashamed. She panics, bursts into tears, and runs away from the assembly. In her mind, she is now a failure. A tiny gremlin hatches in Anne that day. It is a voice that says' You are not good at speaking in front of people. Maybe you should not embarrass yourself like this again."

After this experience, Anne never comes forward to give a public speech. Every time an opportunity to present comes along, the gremlin voice tells her that it is not safe for her to do so. The gremlin is Anne's protector.

Fast forward to her adult life. Anne is now a young lady working in an office. The memory of the school assembly has faded away. She is a hard worker who has proven herself in her chosen career. One day, her boss comes up to her and informs her that her hard work has earned her a promotion as a team leader. While she is thrilled, she is also terrified. Anne does not know why, but a big part of her is resisting the offer. Her gremlin, which subconsciously suspects that her team leader role will involve presenting information in public settings, is trying to protect her. The voice she hears in her is, "You cannot take this on. You will make a fool of yourself if you do. You are not good enough for this promotion."

Unfortunately, Anne does not know where the voice is coming from. She cannot separate the gremlin voice from her personality. She is confused about her lack of confidence, and her confusion feeds her gremlin. Ultimately, Anne decides to forgo the promotion, feeling like a failure, and never having confronted her gremlin.

All of us have gremlins and multiple gremlins at that. The voices come to us in many ways, and even though they are designed to look like voices of reason and protection, they are not compassionate. We cannot wish away our gremlins. The only thing to do is acknowledge that these gremlins are real and engage in dialog. As a coach, I encourage people to understand their gremlins and treat them with compassion. After all, our gremlins are a part of us. I sometimes ask my coachees to visualize their gremlins and have conversations with them. And when the gremlins have had their say, I ask my coachees to thank the gremlins and ask them to kindly move on. Self-compassion takes over the space that gremlins had occupied.

Here are some examples of gremlin voices and how you can replace them with voices of self-compassion.

Self Compassion Dialogs

Gremlin Voice	Compassion Voice

Illusions

Who needs self-compassion? I am strong. Self compassion is for the weak.	Self compassion is oxygen for the mind and soul. Everyone needs it. My perception of strong and weak has nothing to do with my need for self compassion.

Self Worth

I need to meet some imaginary standard of excellence to feel worthy.	There is only one standard for excellence. Me. If I am a little better today than yesterday, I am in the excellence track.

Forgiveness

Forgiving is forgetting. If I forgive I become a weaker person. I do injustice to my hurts by forgiving.	Forgiving is choosing to lose my chains. When I lose my chains I travel faster and farther. Regrets and hurts are only lenses to see my reality- they are not my reality.

Priorities

In my current phase in life, I cannot afford to prioritize me. Taking time for myself is taking away time from my family and work.	Self compassion is no less essential for my well being than sleeping or eating. It is true that I can save time by not eating or sleeping, but I will burn out and crash very quickly.

Clinging

I must hold onto negative experiences to avoid being hurt	I do not have to place emotional content on experiences to remember. Clinging is placing emotional content on outcomes I cannot control. I am wasting precious emotional space by clinging

Fear

If I do not constantly push myself, I will lose out	When I constantly push myself, I lose my balance. To know why and when I push myself helps me find balance. To look inside and know myself is my greatest act of courage

"Self-compassion is like a muscle. The more we practice flexing it, especially when life doesn't go exactly according to plan (a frequent scenario for most of us), the stronger and more resilient our compassion muscle becomes."
— Sharon Salzberg, Real Love: The Art of Mindful Connection

Guilt

I do not deserve kindness. If I do, I am a selfish person.	There is nothing selfish about taking care of myself. If I don't, I undermine the power that trusted my consciousness to this body. If I cannot give myself kindness, I cannot give anyone else kindness sustainably.

Stress

Life is meant to be stressful. More stress means more success.	A little bit of stress challenges me to grow. Too much stress burns me out. Life is not meant to be stressful. Life is meant to be a fearless exploration of personal truths.

Anger

Its okay to be angry at myself as long as my anger does not hurt anyone else.

Anger is negative energy. Anger is acid that eats away its container, and spews out into the open. Whether my anger is directed toward myself or others, the damage to me is real.

Comparison

If I do not compare myself to others, how can I further myself. Envy that comes from comparison hurts me, but that's normal.

Being inspired by others' and comparing myself to others are different things. In comparing to others, I judge my self worth. Envy clouds wisdom, and pushes me toward behaviors that I am not proud of

Whole self

What does self compassion have to do with eating right, exercising and looking good?

My body, my mind and my spirit are all equal components of the person that I am. I need to nurture all of me to be and stay happy. Self-compassion is not a concept. It is a holistic way of being

Procrastination

I have a busy enough life now. Maybe, at a later stage in my life, I will have the time to explore self compassion.

If I practice self compassion, I will open up so much more time and space in my everyday life. This will help me achieve more, and be less busy

Indulgence

Of course I am self compassionate. I love ice cream. I ate two tubs of icecream in one sitting last night!

Self indulgence is rooted in greed. Self compassion is rooted in balance. Self indulgence is self destructive. Self compassion is rooted in awareness and foresight.

LETTING GO OF NEGATIVE MEMORIES

Letting go of negative memories is not easy. It is not easy because then we are asking to let go of our illusion of control. But it requires acts of letting go to experience life fully.

There is a Buddhist tale of a man who was walking through the forest lost in thought. All of a sudden, a tiger starter starts chasing him. He runs and runs, and accidentally slips from a mountain cliff. Fortunately, as he is falling, he reaches out and manages to grab a tree root that is projecting from the mountainside. Unfortunately, a pair of mice start to gnaw on the roots. The man looks up and sees the tiger waiting to eat him above. He looks down and sees the great chasm waiting to swallow him below. He looks at the roots that are holding him from death, and he looks at the two mice that are nibbling away at his final hope. Realizing that there is no escape, he looks around and sees a beautiful red strawberry near him. He reaches out for the strawberry with one hand and pops it in his mouth. And it was the most delicious thing he had ever tasted.

The human brain has a bias for negativity. When good things happen, we feel good. When bad things happen, we feel bad. But the bad feelings last much longer than the good feelings. We have Velcro brains. Negative experiences have the right type of hooks to stick to brain Velcro, and they don't come off easily.

There is an evolutionary advantage to remembering negative experiences. The antelope in the savannah, which saw a member of his group killed, found it advantageous to remember the incident, so he would not end up a victim. Most of the lions in our current life are long dead, but our brains do not know the difference between real and dead lions.

Negative memories create guilt, anger, and fear. So they initiate the same survival response – inflammatory chemicals fill our bodies, we lose sleep, and cell cycles go out of whack. There is disease, and there is suffering. One of the symbolic ways to work with letting go of negative memories is to create a **let-go box**. Here is how a let-go box works:

1. Next time a negative memory comes up, write it down on a piece of paper. Avoid the urge to go off on tangents and try to be as specific as you can about the memory.

2. Be honest about your feelings around this memory. After all, this is for your eyes only.

3. Remind yourself of the common humanity of mistake making. Remember that given a choice today, you would not likely be letting situations the way they unfolded to create your negative memory.

4. Thank the memory for all that it has made out of you. Acknowledge that like all things this memory has to go. Now that it is submitted to the universe, you are free to let go of the memory.

5. Put the paper into a private box.

6. When it is time, burn up the paper, with the understanding that you are taking away the power and sway the memory holds upon you.

The memory may come back, but if you have put the right energy into it, you will find that the emotional impact of the memory is lessened or even lost.

FORGIVENESS

Forgiving someone who has wronged us is one of the most courageous things to do. How can you forgive someone who has ruined your life with his/her malice and callousness? How can you forgive someone who abused you in your most vulnerable moments and took away your faith in people? There are no right answers, except that I believe it is possible to forgive even the worst of transgressions. There are examples to prove this.

One of the most notorious serial killers of our time is Gary Ridgway, dubbed as the Green River Killer. He confessed to the killing of 48 people, although the actual number of his victims is not clear. During his trial, the relatives of his victims came forward to give their victim impact statements. Understandably, every victim impact statement was filled with bitterness, anger, and hate; people wished him pain and suffering in every possible way. Ridgway sat through the trial stone-faced, almost disinterested. And then the father of one of the victims came up and said this:

'Mr. Ridgway, there are people here that hate you. But I am not one of them. You have made it difficult for me to live up to what I believe, and that is what God says to do, and that is to forgive. You are forgiven, sir."

At this, Gary Ridgway, the killer who had not shown any remorse throughout the proceedings, broke down and cried[3].

The possibility of forgiveness happens when we realize that we forgive not for the sake of others, but ourselves. With forgiveness, we can move forward lighter and in peace. In the process of forgiveness, we are performing a powerful act of self-compassion. But as is always the direction of compassion, it becomes imperative to strengthen our fences against future transgressions. While we take away the emotional content about the experience and the person who hurt us by forgiving, we also need to remember the experience and prevent them from happening again.

Nelson Mandela spent twenty-seven years in jail, most of it on the notorious Robben Island off Cape Town, after South Africa's high court found him and his cohorts guilty of having conspired to overthrow the government on June 1964. Even though the most precious years of his life had been unjustly stolen from him, he found the heart to forgive. He said this about his release: *"As I walked out the door toward the gate that would lead to my freedom, I knew if I didn't leave my bitterness and hatred behind, I'd still be in prison."*

Who are three people in my life that I need to forgive now to lighten my emotional baggage? How will my forgiveness manifest?

_____

_____

_____

_____

_____

_____

_____

_____

_____

_____

_____

_____

_____

_____

_____

PROMOTING SELF-COMPASSION AS AN INFLUENCER

Being in the workplace allows us the opportunity to influence others with our thoughts and actions and be likewise influenced. Allowing people to become self-compassionate and facilitating their journey into self-compassion can be one of the greatest lifetime gifts we can give our colleagues. Here are some ideas to promote self-compassion in your work setting.

Lead by example. When you practice being kinder and friendlier to yourself, it will show in your demeanor. Your colleagues will notice that your yes's and no's come from a place of authenticity and strength, and they will respect you for it. One of the inclinations of the human mind is that it always desires what someone else has. So when your self-compassion journey makes you balanced, kind, powerful, and free, your colleagues will see it and want some of it too. You will subconsciously permit them to be self-compassionate.

If you are a leader who is in a position to influence the time and work patterns of the people in your organization, you could use that opportunity to promote self-compassionate behaviors. One of these is to become an evangelist of self-compassion by bringing awareness to the topic. Create learning opportunities, create forums for sharing experiences, and help people feel safe enough to be bold and honest.

Self-compassion creates balance. If your leadership role allows you to reward and un-reward workplace behaviors, you can use it as an opportunity to promote self-compassion. Think of the person on your team who is so obsessed with perfection that she is unable to move forward: you can give her a reality check on perfectionism. Think of the two team members who have been locked in ego-battles for months and are unable to let go of their gripe and return to harmony- you can create opportunities for mediation of conflict. Encourage those who take care of their bodies through exercise, instead of categorizing it as a personal preference. Encouraging someone does not mean bias or putting anyone else down- fairness is giving credit where credit is due.

Un-incentivize unhealthy competition. A famous scientist in an Ivy League university has this practice of pitting his post-doctoral fellows against each other. He gives the same research topic to two of his post-doctoral fellows and tells them that whoever can complete the project first will get a life-changing publication and the other will lose out everything. You can imagine the kind of competition that this directive sets off. A distinct lack of self-compassion and compassion is seen in his lab. Researchers have had other lab members steal data, forcing them to lock up their lab books when they step out. Researchers in the lab work inhuman hours to win the race, ignoring their body's needs. Some postdoctoral fellows cozy up to their boss so they can get an advantage come publication time. This scientist may be famous and an expert in his field, but in my opinion, he is an example of everything that a leader should not be. If you have the capacity to influence self-compassion in your work, un-incentivizing unhealthy competition can be a great way to make it happen.

What are some steps I can do as an influencer in my current job setting to promote self-compassion?

_____

_____

_____

_____

_____

_____

_____

_____

_____

_____

_____

_____

TIPS AND TOOLS FOR SELF-COMPASSION

"I am not perfect; I am not invulnerable. I, like everyone else, experience suffering. But I notice my limitations without judgment. I accept and grow with my experiences. I exercise my capacity for kindness."

Here are some ideas that could help your self-compassion journey.

- Keep a journal of the negative self-criticism and self-defeating thoughts over two days. Identify a partner to share your notes with at the end of the exercise. Would you say these to a good friend? What does this mean for you?
- Remind yourself that if you cannot treat yourself kindly, no one else can

- Remind yourself that you deserve kindness irrespective of who, what, where, why, and when
- Write a compassionate letter to self in the third person as if you were writing to your best friend. Write down your counsel, aspirations, and wishes for you.
- Create a self-compassion statement and keep it in view to remind yourself
- Remember that you are not alone.
- Surround yourself with positive people
- Do the mirror exercise. **Coach Santalynda Marrero** shares this personal self-compassion exercise that she uses to break from judgment:

"**B**efore I walk out of my home, I stand in front of the mirror and point to my reflection and pick myself apart." Look at you" I tell my reflection "your hair is graying, your skin is sagging, you have a pimple on your nose that looks ugly" After I have ripped myself apart, I pause and turn the finger onto myself, and say "But you, you are nothing like that reflection. You are perfect. Your body, mind, and spirit are as beautiful as they are." And then, in the knowledge that I am as perfect as I am meant to be, I step out to face my day. Before you start your day, stand in front of a mirror, point to the reflection, and pour out your criticism. When the catharsis is over, point to your real self and heap all the platitudes you deserve."

- If appropriate, experiment with healthier eating. There is a Tamil saying which goes, 'Food is medicine; medicine is food.' Try out the 'hara hachi bu' principle from Okinawa, Japan, which advises that you stop eating when you are 80% full. Eating only when hungry, and stopping when still a little bit hungry, is a sure shot way to a healthier you.
- Plan to give away something physical you have been hoarding, but not using. Commit not to replace it with more baggage. Observe your emotions after you let go of the physical object. Do you experience loss, relief, anxiety, or space?

- Think of an emotional baggage that you have been lugging around. Visualize how you would feel to let go of that emotional baggage. Would you experience loss, relief, anxiety, or space? Experiment with discarding your emotional baggage.

MY KEY TAKEAWAYS FROM THIS CHAPTER

_____
_____
_____
_____
_____
_____
_____
_____
_____
_____
_____
_____
_____
_____
_____
_____
_____

People First Thinking?

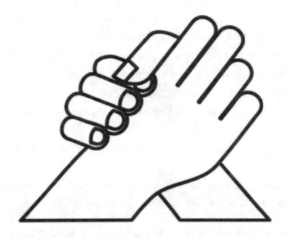

Why people-first thinking?

When we stop seeing people as assets and start viewing them as valuable collaborators, it becomes easy for us to be compassionate to them. This means treating people with fairness and respect. It means not being opportunistic, being sensitive to the possibility that our actions might hurt our colleagues. It also means a willingness to prioritize people over business outcomes if needed. It also means that, in our role as influencers, we consistently prioritize people, and we inspire trust. In this process, we create a work setting where people feel safe enough to thrive, innovate, and collaborate.

In this chapter, we discuss why people-first thinking matters, how to create a people-first mindset, and how to use the mindset as an influencer to create compassionate change in our work settings.

People first thinking brings out the best in people. It comes from the awareness that every person we meet is deserving of the same dignity, respect, and compassion as ourselves, no matter what. People first thinkers avoid dehumanizing people by binning them as statistics. They resist the temptation to be opportunistic, because of an innate sense of fairness tells them that if they were on the receiving end, that is not how they would like to be treated.

Try having a vulnerable reflection of the questions below to understand your take on people-first thinking.

- Do I see the people you lead as resources?
- How much do I know of their 'human' face?
- How well do I listen to people I influence?
- How much value do I show for the personal needs of the people I influence?
- If I am in a leadership role, how do I treat them when they make mistakes?
- If I am a leader, how do I support their long term growth, outside of their role in the organization?

What do you answers reveal about how you prioritize people?

_____

_____

_____

_____

_____

_____

_____

_____

_____

_____

_____

_____

_____

_____

Making people feel valued

Maya Angelou said,

> "I've learned that people will forget what you said, people will forget what you did, but people will never forget how you made them feel."

Ultimately, it all comes down to how we feel and how we make people think.

Have you had a people-first thinking leader in your work life who made you feel exceptional? This is a person who made you feel like you mattered. You knew this person had your back and would never throw you under the bus for personal gain. This person made you want to dig deep into your personal reserves and show up as the best version of yourself.

Have you also had a leader in your life for whom you were only a resource or a number? Being in this person's space made you fearful and disrespected. You always felt that this person had ulterior motives and was using you for their personal gain. This leader made you feel small and worthless and filled you with self-doubt.

Consider the situation of a layoff.

At Company A, an employee comes to work but finds his key card is not working. He walks to the HR to complain but is told that he has been laid off and he has an hour to pack his things and leave. A security guard stays with him for that period, making sure he does not steal any proprietary information. Since all his colleagues are watching, the employee feels ashamed and humiliated, but there is nothing he can do. There are no goodbyes, and he is summarily escorted out. The company justifies that this is the right thing to do to preserve sensitive information and to prevent demoralizing conversations by the person being laid off.

At Company B, an employee is informed in person by his manager about the extenuating circumstances in which he is being let go. The manager is kind and considerate and offers support during the process. When the employee meets HR, there is more support and offers for outplacement support (support between jobs), including connections to recruiters. The employee is given enough time to wind down, plan, and say goodbyes. There is respect all around, and the employee leaves with dignity.

The above two situations are real examples. The shortsightedness of Company A lies in that people who have been ill-treated will have only negative things to share about their company in their social world. And we live in a Glassdoor world, where job seekers make their choices based on what reviews they read online. And also there is the observer effect, where people who witness this kind of tough layoff are demoralized. They realize that it could very well be them being treated that way. And so they start looking out for opportunities elsewhere where they will be treated with more respect and dignity. Not having people first mindset as an organization is a sure-shot way to cause talent drain.

You do not have to be in a leadership role to practice people first thinking. Irrespective of your role in your organization, you can choose to exercise the people-first mindset. This mindset shows up in small but powerful ways. How we acknowledge people, and how we treat people when they are in trouble, how we stand up for people who are being bullied in our workplaces and more. The human impact of people-first mindset is always enormous.

Coach Santalynda Marrero shares this experience.

"Several years ago, I worked in a hospital system. My role was to manage funding for social initiatives. Very often, the top executives of our organization would be present in these meetings. If the cleaning lady ever walked into these meetings to clean the trash, I made it a point to thank her by name. At that time, it was not the status quo to address janitors by name. But I knew that for the cleaning lady, it felt good to be acknowledged in front of the executive team. Eventually, the CEO of the company sitting in the meetings noticed the message of inclusiveness I was trying to get across, and he too started acknowledging the cleaning lady and thereby leveling the playing field.**"**

People first thinking requires a healthy dose of courage and integrity. When there are so many competing priorities, it is easy to put business interests over people. We are taught to believe that throwing people under the bus in lieu of shareholder interest is the right thing to do. We are taught that it is normal to step on people's toes to climb up the ladder of professional success. To shift to people-first thinking is to turn away from these popular narratives. It is not easy, but certainly doable. And in the bigger scheme of life, it pays human dividends.

Coach Santalynda Marrero shares yet another life experience about this.

"**O**ne of the executives of my organization took a special interest in my work. One day, she called me aside and suggested that I take over the role of leading a particularly high profile project. She felt my approach and education would help move the project forward faster than under its current leadership. It felt good for my ego to be asked. But I also knew that my colleague leading the project had invested a good deal of her time and energy in the project. I asked myself how it would feel for me to be in her position - to be side-stepped in favor of a colleague. I told the executive that I was thankful for her consideration, but the only way I would consider taking this on was as a co--leader of the project. The executive was initially reluctant, but she let me have my way. I then approached my colleague, and praised her for her efforts on the project and then asked if she would feel comfortable if I co-led the project with her. I never told her about the executive's suggestion. Happily, for me, she was excited at the idea. With her experience and my insight, the project turned out to be very successful. But more importantly, she became a very dear friend to me. Even after I moved on from the organization and even after she has retired from work, our friendship continues.

Recently she and I were having tea when out of the blue, she said,

"Santa, you remember the project we worked on all those years ago?"

I nodded, yes.

"I never told you this,' she said slowly, "but I know what you did, and I love you for it."

In pausing to be compassionate and inclusive, not only had I found a workplace collaborator, but I had gained a life-long friend. **"**

The question then is, how can we create the people first mindset?

The first thing is to identify what is blocking us from prioritizing people in our lives. It could be that we are so ingrained in the social narrative that numbers matter more than people. Or we could be short-sighted in that we believe that people are less important than immediate personal growth goals. Or it could simply be a lack of skills in taking perspectives (we will see more of this in the Big-picture thinking chapter). Whatever the case is, if we can be so courageous as to look at our own lack, we will then be empowered to work on it.

So here is a self-reflection exercise:

What opportunities do I have to practice the people-first mindset in my workplace?

_____

_____

_____

_____

_____

_____

_____

_____

_____

_____

_____

_____

_____

Below, we will discuss some of the essential elements of the people-first mindset and tools we can use to make it a part of our everyday work life.

People first thinking promotes psychological safety

Just a few years ago, Google published the results of its **Project Aristotle** that had been studying workplace values and behaviors that contribute to the most successful teams in its offices globally[4]. At the top of the list was 'psychological safety'- a word coined by Dr. Amy Edmondson at the Harvard Business School in her works. Dr. Edmondson defines psychological safety as "a sense of confidence that the team will not embarrass, reject or punish someone for speaking up[5]". Inc. magazine describes psychological safety as 'a situation in which everyone is safe to take risks, voice their opinions, and ask judgment-free questions. A culture where managers provide air cover and create safe zones so employees can let down their guard.[6]'

Why is it so important for people to feel safe in their workplace? Because that is the difference between bringing their full presence to the workplace versus not. Psychologically safe employees are willing to be more engaged and invested in their work because they know that their voices are valued and their opinions matter. Because they are aligned to the bigger goals and vision of their company, they notice when things are amiss. Since they trust (trust in this context is how we believe people will treat us and our opinions) that pointing out their concerns will not result in personal retaliation or how they are perceived and treated by their leaders and team members, they feel emboldened to point out their concerns.

A friend of mine had a very difficult time during her Ph.D. years. Her advisor was an egoistic man who demanded absolute compliance. If anyone in his lab pointed out a mistake in his work, he would become defensive and humiliate them in lab meetings. The only reason why my friend and all the other students in the lab persisted was the dream of a doctoral degree, which was under the discretion of the boss. After eight years of struggle, my friend managed to complete her thesis, but soon after decided to pursue a non-science career. She told me that one of the most difficult decisions she had to make was toward the end of her doctoral program. Her research was about small RNAs in cancer tissues.

Cindy W (Name changed)
Journalist

"Somewhere in the seventh year of my thesis, I made this remarkable discovery. Purely coincidental, but it seemed I had discovered a novel explanation for a cellular phenomenon that the research field was trying to decode. I was thrilled, but I did not want to share this discovery with my boss. I knew his first instinct would be to put me down. I knew that much about him after working with him for six-plus years. Then he would manipulate me to stay on in his lab, being the senior student in his lab. That meant my Ph.D. would be delayed by a few more years. As interesting as my science was, my bitter experience being in his lab had already convinced me that I was not going to continue in science. I was torn for a while, but I also did not want to sacrifice what was important for me, my self-esteem, and my timelines, for the sake of science and certainly not for him. Since the discovery was not directly related to my thesis, I quietly swept my discovery under the rug. If the lab had pursued this, they would have become scientific superstars, with all the publications and grants that would have come their way. I know this because a couple of years later, another lab reported the finding in a high impact journal. This lab did become a superstar lab because of the report. I sometimes wonder how different it would have been if my boss had been a less egoistic, more caring person. It would have been a win-win for all of us."

In discussing psychological safety in healthcare, Dr. Edmondson talks about three things that need to be done[7]:

1. Framing the work (emphasizing on the meaningfulness of the work, and laying out challenges in the open)
2. Being fallible as leaders and asking for feedback
3. Embracing Messengers (thanking people for their points of view)

Psychological safety is tied to innovation. Innovation happens when you can take an existing product or idea to a higher level of application. Innovation requires that memories, experiences, and learning come together around an existing product or idea to create novel solutions for unmet needs. For us to create this much complexity, some needs must be met.

- First, we must perceive a purpose in innovating.
- Second, our brain must not be distracted by survival stresses. (Think of the Maslowian hierarchy of needs. Self-actualization happens only when physiological and psychological needs are met).
- Finally, we must feel psychologically safe in innovating and sharing our innovation.

Imagine that I am an assembly line worker in a car manufacturing plant, working long hours with basic pay. With the existing protocol, it takes me two hours to complete my assigned assembly for each car. But based on my instinct and long experience, I know this protocol can be improved, and I can potentially save valuable assembly time. The idea of me creating something novel is appealing. I experiment with the protocol in my downtime and realize that modifying the sequence will help me complete my assigned task in one hour instead of two. This would be a significant value addition to the company since there are three hundred other workers like me. Even though I am excited and want to share this development with my supervisor, I ask myself: Do I trust my supervisor enough to be fair and give me due credit? Even if he takes on the idea, will he give the time relief, which my innovation is supposed to create (more autonomy, work fewer hours)?

Unless my relationship with my supervisor is one of trust and safety, and unless my survival needs are adequately addressed, my instinct could be

To not care about innovation. I could merely be a cog in the machine and get paid, so that is what I would do.

Or I might innovate because I am curious, but not share it because I do not trust my boss

Or if I innovate, I might take my innovation to a different company if my company does not meet my financial needs.

Organizations can lose out extraordinary innovation opportunities by not providing them the right conditions to think, explore, and express their creativity.

People first thinking promotes fairness

Primatologist and Ethologist **Frans de Waal** has demonstrated that the need for fairness holds true for monkeys, dogs, chimpanzees, and other animals[8]. Two trained capuchin monkeys were placed side by side in cages. The monkeys had been taught to complete a task (i.e., give a rock to the researcher) to earn a reward. The rewards were either cucumbers or grapes. Capuchin monkeys prefer grapes to cucumbers by a wide margin. The two monkeys complete their tasks, both get a reward of cucumbers, and they are happy. But when one of them receives a cucumber, and she sees that her friend is receiving a grape for the same task, she becomes very agitated. She throws away her cucumber and starts banging on her cage in evident angst.

What is true of capuchin monkeys is true for us.

Abdul Kalam, the beloved former president of India, dubbed as India's 'Missile Man' shared an example of great leadership from his boss, Professor Satish Dhawan. In August 1979, India was all prepared to enter the space age with the launch of its first Satellite Launch Vehicle (SLV). Dr.Kalam was the project director of the mission, and Dr. Dhawan was the Chairman of the Indian Space Research Agency. The launch of the SLV was a moment of great pride for India, so there was much expectation and media coverage. As the countdown for the launch started, the computer put the launch on hold. There was a leak. The group of scientists with Dr. Kalam did their calculations and assured him that the issue was minor and the computer could be bypassed. Dr. Kalam, as head of the mission, had to make a critical decision, and he did. He bypassed the computer controls and launched the SLV. The first phase of the SLV worked well, but the second phase failed and the SLV instead of heading to space, crashed into the ocean. Soon afterward, Dr. Dhawan led a press meet, with Dr. Kalam present. Instead of throwing his team under the bus as he very well could have, Dr. Dhawan took responsibility for the failure and assured the press that he believed in his team and that the next time they would undoubtedly be successful.

Dr. Dhawan's faith in them motivated the scientists to work harder than ever before. In less than a year from that incident, the team, once again headed by Dr. Kalam, launched India's first successful satellite. It was a great victory for the country. This time, at the press conference, Dr. Dhawan asked Dr. Kalam to take over, ensuring that Dr. Kalam and his team, not himself, got the due credits and recognition. It would have been easy for Dr. Dhawan to blame Dr. Kalam during failure, and take credit during success. But Dr. Dhawan made a fair choice, and that influenced a man who would in his life become known for fairness and servant leadership.

Fairness avoids conflict. Fairness promotes trust.

To practice fairness, leaders must avoid picking favorites. When someone who does not deserve appreciation or credit is selected for a promotion or an award simply because they have a better relationship with a supervisor, the other key contributors in the team lose any motivation to perform. On the part of a leader, it takes a certain level of intuition to look past personal biases to identify and reward the most deserving people in the team.

Active Listening is part of people first thinking

Perhaps the greatest gift we can give people is our time. If we are giving of our time to listen to someone, it makes sense to give it wholeheartedly and make every moment count.

We are all storytellers. We are all living stories. We love stories.

When someone comes to us to share his or her story, it is a privilege, not a distraction. Why then should we miss the opportunity to learn and grow through it?

People often confuse listening and hearing. Hearing is an activity of the ears. Listening is an activity of the heart.

Hearing Vs Listening

Hearing	Listening
Is about the listener	Is about the speaker
Little emotional content	Active emotional content
Deeper intent of conversation is often lost. The non-verbal language and the subliminal messages are missed.	Deeper intent of conversation is not lost. The non-verbal language and the subliminal messages are noted.
Does not make the speaker feel valued	Makes the speaker feel valued
Curiosity is missing	Active curiosity
Listener is thinking about response, not about understanding	Listener is thinking about understanding, not about response
Conversations are interrupted, there is a feeling of incompleteness.	Conversations flow effortlessly, feeling of completeness.

Active listening enables us to be a part of someone's story.

Friends who have had the opportunity to talk to His Holiness the Dalai Lama share that in the time that you spend with him, he makes you feel like you are the most important person in the world. He listens with childlike curiosity, intent and earnestness that makes you feel like the most special person in the world. I have heard this being said of a few other extraordinary human beings as well. I have also heard that these masters of listening have the skill of creating elegant boundaries. Great listeners know the art of providing emotional content to the conversation but not entangling themselves emotionally with the pain of the speaker. They also know the art of saying no when needed, when it is no longer self-compassionate or sustainable to do so. Great listening is compassion in action- noticing, feeling, suspending judgment, and trying to identify opportunities to alleviate pain.

People-first thinking is tough compassion

To put people first does not mean compromising on business goals or being a pushover to accommodate people, or overlook their faults, or not give tough feedback. As with all compassion practices, the intent of putting people first is built on intent for their success and happiness and can manifest as tough love. If my intent as a leader is to help my colleague shine in her role, I should be prepared to give tough, authentic feedback if my colleague is not doing her tasks well. I would do it with great kindness, but I would not hesitate to let my colleague know that things need improving. Also, people first thinking does not mean my shareholders need to suffer. But keeping the idea of people first thinking as an undercurrent of thought helps temper difficult decisions with compassion.

People first thinking creates amazing
human experiences

Like all of the other pillars of compassion, people-first thinking inspires others to act compassionately. A good leader sets the tone for fairness in his team. A leader of an organization who promotes psychological safety inspires team leaders to create psychological safety in their teams. Active listeners inspire others to reciprocate in kind. When a group of people with people-first thinking come together, incredible experiences are created.

Ferose VR
Senior Vice President, SAP Labs Silicon Valley

"While I was the managing director at SAP Labs India, all the Operations teams (HR, Admin, Facilities, IT, Finance) reported into me. This team was responsible for ensuring the smooth functioning of the entire 4000+ people organization. The team had around 120 people (many of them working as contract employees). Every year, we had a tradition of doing a 2-3 day offsite meeting to drive the mission and objectives for the year. It was also an occasion for the entire team to come together as ONE team. In 2011, the team decided to do the event in Colombo in SriLanka. The default thinking was that only the permanent employees would participate and not the ones who were working as contractors. Most of the contractors were doing the job of janitors (functions like housekeeping, cleaning, packaging, mail delivery, etc.). Much against the practice, we decided that everyone would travel together. The budget was not enough, and most of the contract employees did not even have a passport. The leadership decided that they would put the money from their own pockets to ensure that everyone had a chance to be together. The teams worked together to ensure that passports and VISA were taken for the contract employees. It was an event of a lifetime; many boarding a flight for the first time. The team was proud that an entire flight was booked and everyone – from the Managing Director to the Janitor went together. Even after many years, everyone still remembers the spirit in which such an event took place – what really made it special was that we treated everyone with compassion and as equals. We broke some rules, but never compromised on our principles!"

People-first thinking is a power tool in customer service interactions as well. Going into customer interactions helps service providers create meaningful experiences for their clients, thereby improving customer satisfaction and loyalty.

Amuthan Sundar
Senior Business Analyst

"Several years ago, I was handling customer calls for the night shift in Citibank. A customer called me in the early hours of the morning. He had lost his credit card and had called during the day. But on that particular day, there had been a technical issue, and his case had somehow fallen between the cracks. He was evidently angry, and he was yelling into the phone. It was a charged moment. They say the customer is always right, but it is not always easy to remember that when the attacks are personal. But at that moment, I somehow managed to pause and ask myself this question- 'How would I feel if I were in his position? What would I love to hear that will make me feel better?' That simple act of perspective taking stopped me from being reactive at the moment. I managed to talk to him calmly and clearly, expressing my genuine concern for his situation. I told him that I would immediately initiate the cancellation of his card and work on reissuing a new card. I also assured him that he would have nothing to worry about as far as his card was concerned. It was a simple, authentic human act because, at that moment, I was not working with a phone number, but a human being like me who was under duress. Somehow, my conversation with him must have impacted him deeply. He wrote about his positive experience to Citibank soon after this event. As a result, Citibank honored me with an award for that year. All it took was for me to see this customer as a person in need of help at a time of distress.**"

Promoting people-first thinking as a leader

People-first thinking, as a pillar of compassion, is particularly useful as a leadership practice. Here are some ideas to practice people-first thinking in your leadership role:

- Always initiate conversations with curiosity for their well-being
- Be genuinely concerned, be respectful always
- Listen, don't just hear. Here is a short group exercise to try in your next team meeting. Pair people up in your team. One person talks for two minutes, and the other person observes and acknowledges, bringing their full interest and presence to those two minutes. The listener should try not to make any judgments, but recognize that its the other person's story.
- Giving authentic feedback
- Let people know that they are valued
- Consistently treat people with fairness.

How can I, as a leader and influencer, promote people first thinking in my current work setting?

_____

_____

_____

_____

_____

_____

_____

_____

_____

_____

_____

_____

_____

_____

_____

MY KEY TAKEAWAYS FROM THIS CHAPTER

_____

_____

_____

_____

_____

_____

_____

_____

_____

_____

_____

_____

_____

_____

_____

_____

_____

_____

_____

_____

Abundance Mindset

"Stop acting so small. You are the universe in ecstatic motion." -**Rumi**

What is the abundance mindset?

Let us start this pillar of compassion with a short self-assessment.

Try to answer each question with a **Y**-Yes, **N**-No or **M**-Maybe.

1. I see my world as a place with limited resources and opportunities
2. If I have the resources or information that can benefit others, I use it to leverage personal power
3. I suspect that people are after me and my resources
4. The success of my friends makes me envious
5. I cannot get myself to appreciate people wholeheartedly
6. I see my interactions are transactional. My go-to mindset is 'what is in it for me?'

7. If I do not see myself gaining anything through my efforts, I would likely not do them.
8. I see the world as an increasingly competitive and unsustainable place.
9. I avoid making bets on people because humans are unpredictable.

How many Yes's, No's and Maybe's did you end up with. What are some answers you would want to see changed?

The objective of this quick assessment was not to be judgmental, but for you to bring awareness to the blocks you may be facing with abundance thinking.

Abundance is a mindset, not the presence or absence of physical wealth. Abundance stems from a place of deep trust and fearlessness. Abundance thinking allows us to act as the best versions of ourselves because we know that the world we live in is an unlimited, generous place. Our world as we know is what it is because of the abundance of countless heroes. Yet, most of us subscribe to the idea of scarcity. Evolutionarily we have had to compete for resources. For perhaps the first time in human history, a significant portion of the human race has access to an abundance of opportunities and resources. However, the evolutionary fears of scarcity and insecurity persist and stop us from sharing freely and abundantly.

Until a vaccine was discovered in 1953, polio was one of the most dreaded diseases in the world. Hundreds of thousands of children were becoming paralyzed every year because of polio. But just a few years later the number of polio cases had dramatically dropped. By 2013, The World Health Organization reported only 416 reported cases of polio worldwide. The person who developed the polio vaccine was Jonas Salk. Edward R. Murrow, a TV journalist, asked Salk who owned the polio vaccine patent. "Well, the people, I would say," Salk responded. "There is no patent. Could you patent the sun?" Neither he nor Albert Sabin, the scientist who discovered the alternate version of the polio vaccine claimed a patent for their discoveries[9]. If the polio vaccine had been patented, the world would have added a couple more billionaires but lost countless millions to the disease.

Scarcity breeds fear and prevents the sharing of resources. The message of scarcity is everywhere. Every advertisement out there reminds you that you lack something. Marketers tell us that their products are on 'a limited time offer' and unless we act within a specific timeframe, we will lose out. Product, pricing, promotion, and distribution strategies are carefully designed to make us want something immediately because they are difficult to obtain. The FOMO- fear of missing out- is so accepted that no one questions the motivations of these marketing campaigns anymore. Thanksgiving sales, for example, are built on the foundations of scarcity. We accept that unless we rush and scramble early on Thanksgiving, we will miss out on a very limited supply of 'doorbuster specials'. It is sad to see people trampling over each other, ignoring the suffering of fellow human beings, for the mad rush of financial gain.

What scarcity thinking do I currently subscribe to? How does it stop me from being as expansive as I can be?

_____
_____
_____
_____
_____
_____
_____
_____
_____
_____
_____
_____
_____
_____

Why abundance mindset?

Eckhart Tolle, author of 'Power of Now', says *"Acknowledging the good that you already have in your life is the foundation for all abundance."* Abundance stems from gratitude and acknowledging that we are conduits of universal goodness- a temporary pipeline through which knowledge and resources flow. Either we can be a good conduit for the universe to flow through us, or we can resist and try to hold on to what flows through us. Imagine a blood vessel that says, "I cannot let all the fatty goodness pass through me. What do I gain out of just being a pass-through? Going forward, I am going to hold on to the fats and retain them right here" That blood vessel will not just create a clot, but it will also cause a heart attack which will cause a system collapse, including the destruction of the blood vessel that started the problem.

Abundance is a window through which opportunities enter and leave. Seeds of opportunities continuously bombard us. When we practice the scarcity mindset, we keep our windows closed so that none of our precious seeds escape our fold, but in doing so, we also prevent the seeds of opportunities to come into our worlds. When we practice abundance, however, our windows are wide open. And through the same windows that our seeds fly out into the world, others, even more precious, float in. As abundance mindset takes root, psychological safety, fairness, big-picture think-ing manifest in the workplace.

A news reporter traveled to interview a farmer who had won an award for his special cultivar of corn. On his way to meet the farmer, the reporter noticed that not only the farmer's fields but also all of the neighboring fields had the same award-winning corn.

"Of course," said the farmer, when the reporter asked him about this. "I gave the seeds to all my neighbors to grow in their fields."

"Aren't you afraid that one of your neighbors will use your corn to create something even better and win the prize?"

"That they might," the farmer replied. "But what choice do I have? If I refuse to share my seeds, I will have high quality corn on my farm, and they will have low quality corn in theirs. But the wind will blow and the bees will pollinate. My corn will mix with theirs, and theirs will mix with mine. Next year, I will surely end up with poor corn for sure. My chances are better this way."

A great reason to practice abundance is the inevitability that abundance will attract abundance. Brian Tracy, author and speaker, says this: *"You are a living magnet. What you attract into your life is in harmony with your dominant thoughts."*

There is a story of a recently-dead man who was told that he could choose between heaven and hell. He first visited hell, where he saw hordes of hungry, angry residents sitting around an enormous vat of delicious boiling stew. Their hands were fastened to soup ladles with enormously long handles. They could dip into the vat, but could not bring the stew to their mouths because of how they were fastened to their hands. The man then visited heaven, where he saw the exact same arrangements. But the people there seemed to be fell fed and happy. He asked the escorting angel about this curious difference.

'It's quite simple,' replied the angel. 'The ones in heaven figured out that they could reach into the vat, fill it will stew and feed the person on the other side. They acted from abundance and trusted that the other person would reciprocate, and they were right. So now, everyone in heaven feeds everyone else, and no one goes hungry. In hell, they are held back by fear and suspicion. No one is abundant, and everyone goes hungry.'

As a pillar of compassion, abundance is tied to gratitude. The more gratitude we feel, the more we realize how abundant life has been for us, and more compelled we feel to share without holding back. Abundance is driven by love, while fear drives abundance away.

Blocks to abundance mindset

These are some of the blocks to an abundance mindset.

- lack or noticing how much we have (gratitude and abundance go hand in hand)

- small thinking
- agenda based thinking
- win/lose conditioning
- fear of competition
- pessimism about future
- default suspicion

Your next exercise is to look deep and ask-

'What is blocking me from thinking abundantly? What will be different in my thoughts and actions if time, resources, and finances were not limiting?'

_____

_____

_____

_____

_____

_____

_____

_____

_____

_____

_____

_____

_____

_____

Manifestations of abundance thinking

Several years ago, we vacationed at a small town called Fairhope in Alabama - a beautiful quiet town by the Mobile bay. On our way back, we stopped at a coffee shop to stock up on donuts for our way back to New Orleans. After we had ordered and the owner had rung up the price, he instructed us to drop the money in an open moneybox in the shop. Whatever change was due we could simply take from the money bin. This was a busy shop, so people were adding in money and taking out their due change. It was surprising for me to witness this extraordinary setting of trust. When I asked the owner about this unusual arrangement, he laughed and said that that is how it has always been.

'What is someone does not pay for their coffee? Or worse, what if someone takes away money from the money box?'

"We are a small town," he replied. "If anyone needs the money that badly, then they can take it. It is ok. But we have seen that people are fair. If they are short on change, we know they will add it in the next time."

I recently saw another coffee shop based on the same honor system, this time in Valley City in North Dakota. The owner of this coffee shop, The Vault, says that people are 15% more generous than thieving with this arrangement. These honor system based business may or may not be successful in other settings (for example in a big city), but they do provide a ray of hope that abundance need not always be met with disappointment.

One of the greatest social experimenters with abundance that I know of is **Nipun Mehta**. Nipun is the founder of the *'giftivism'* movement, the practice of radically generous acts that transform the world. Giftivism challenges the all too accepted notion that people will always act in self-interest. Giftivism is based on unconditional generosity. Nipun founded **Servicespace** at the height of the dotcom boom to experiment with giftivism. Servicespace volunteers have given away millions of dollars' worth of services building websites, but everything they have provided is a gift. In spite of all skepticism, Servicespace has created its own ecosystem that boasts of more than half-a-million people around the world today. Nipun Mehta's life itself is living proof of abundance. **Karma Kitchen**, which is a part of the Servicespace ecosystem, is a beautiful example of human selflessness. There are 26 Karma Kitchens globally. Run entirely by volunteers, people who eat at Karma Kitchen get a total bill of $0.00, with a note that reads like this: "Your meal was a gift from someone who came before you. To keep the chain of gifts alive, we invite you to pay it forward for those who dine after you."

Nipun's message has spread out, rooted, and inspired abundance all across. Consider this experience narrated by **Birju Pandya**, who is a **Social impact Investor** and an active member of Servicespace.

"**F**inancial success is like the training wheel of the bicycle that needs to come off at some point. There is a story that I like to share. There is a gentleman in the East Coast that I worked with who delivers organic produce to houses. He took on a 21-day kindness challenge through Servicespace. One week into the practice, he told me that he had come to realize that he did not feel connected with his customers. Everything seemed very transactional. As a small step forward, he decided to spend at least one extra minute to connect with his customers. A week later, we were having another phone conversation. He told me that a very interesting thing had occurred to him. He had, as planned, spent the extra minute to talk to a new client, and discovered that the reason she was getting this organic produce was because she had been diagnosed with throat cancer, and she was trying to cure herself. He somehow felt connected with her. He said' I have to do my act of kindness today anyway. So I want to give you this box of vegetables.' It was a 75-dollar box, and it was certainly not financially easy for him to give things away. But he did. As he drove away, he realized that in all the years he had been delivering vegetables, he had never been happier than now. Interestingly, the woman later wrote to him and let him know that she was now his customer for life. Happiness was the outcome; money just happened. And it came from a decision to include a simple practice of kindness. "

Workplaces are exceptional grounds to practice abundance. Before we explore abundance in the context of the workplace, here is an **abundance affirmation** for you to work with:

"I am abundant. I live in a world of abundance. There is plenty to meet my needs and the needs of the world around me. We only need to cultivate the capacity to see common humanity and share freely to create a world of abundance. This abundance starts with me. I share freely without expectations. I enable people with love. I teach others what I know.

I create relationships. I enable people. I operate from a level of higher consciousness. I become bigger and stronger in the process, and doors that I did not know before will open up for my own growth."

Abundance thinking in the Workplace

I saw a cartoon about two executives of a company having a conversation.

What if we train our people and they leave? Says the CFO

What if we do not train them and they stay? Replies the CEO.

There is great suffering in workplaces because of scarcity thinking. Team dynamics are affected greatly when we have some people who are abundant in giving and others who will take but not reciprocate. The tragedy of the commons is a thought experiment that shines light on what happens when many individuals in a community share a limited common resource. If some members of the group become greedy or selfish and take more of the resource than they should, they disrupt the balance and spread the negative effects across the entire community.

Adam Grant, Professor at Wharton Business School, describes three kinds of personalities in the workplace: givers, takers, and matchers. Givers give, Takers take, Matchers wait for others to give and then reciprocate. At the very bottom of organizations are givers, because they have been so busy giving of their time and resources to others that they become doormats. Interestingly, at the very top of the organizational pyramid, also are the givers. This is because, givers, in their sense of abundance, have inspired trust and opened doors for themselves. The difference between the successful givers and the doormat givers are wisdom questions that the successful givers ask and adhere to. What his study shows is that abundance stands the risk of being penalized, and abundance must be paired with a good dose of common sense and wisdom to be sustainable.

As fear blocks abundance and causes withholding information and resources, it is important, if you are in a leadership role, to set the tone for abundance for the people you lead. As a leader, it becomes essential to stop the takers taking undue advantage of the abundance of givers. This becomes a foundation of psychological safety and fairness we saw in the previous chapter. Abundance cannot be consistently practiced from a place of sacrifice. A leader's role is to make sure that there will be enough to go around. For example, scarcity might show up as a person in your team holding back resources to leverage power. Your role as leader would be to discourage those behaviors with honest discussion and modeling behaviors where you do not do the same.

Here is another universal truth I have discovered in my journeys. Abundance mindset can be a power tool in decision-making. *Any major decision made from a place of scarcity is bound to fail. Any major decision made from a place of abundance is destined to succeed.*

To practice sustainable compassion, we must learn to redirect our abundance to where it matters. Redirecting abundance means saying no to some people, opportunities, and information; and saying yes to new perspectives and behaviors.

One of the people I coached was a young woman in the bay area. Tina (name changed) has two young children and a very active social life. In her career, she is a superstar. She has a great relationship with her husband. She used to work 18-hour days, and everyone around her looked up to her for inspiration. She somehow managed to make time for every ask that was posed to her. In her mind, she was a superwoman who could accommodate anything and everything. And so, if she could not meet someone's demand on her time, she would beat herself up for it, and it was taking a toll on her. She was also becoming increasingly dependent on others' validation of her time and presence. The sad part was that she did not realize that most of the people in her life were taking her time for granted, and were feeding her ego to use her. Tina was stretched and burnt out, and her body was in constant pain, but even that made her guilty.

In our coaching sessions, we did some deep work- asking tough questions, facing insecurities face to face, and clarifying priorities. Her breakthrough moment was when she realized that with every 'Yes,' she was saying 'No' to many other more meaningful things in her life. She realized that she could continue to be a truly abundant person, but her abundance would be directed toward the right reasons and people. Boldly, Tina stopped justifying her being a yes-woman and started living her world with true compassion-with power, kindness, and empowerment. She kindly but firmly let her friends know that there were commitments she would not be a part of, because of competing priorities. Judgments and unkind comments from 'friends' followed. Several people dropped out of the radar. But she had gone into this decision from a place of power, so she was able not to personalize the criticism. She took time out for self-nurturing and meditation, and she redirected her abundance to people and efforts that aligned better with her priorities. Magically, as she changed her dialogs and behaviors, the pain in her body began to disappear. She attracted other people who valued her and resonated more with her new presence. Her family was all the more happier because they knew her giving was not coming from a place of sacrifice but a place of excess. Tina had changed her life by redirecting her abundance.

If you are a leader in charge of people, here is a small self-assessment to understand your propensity for abundance.

How abundant is my mindset?

Answer the questions below with a yes or no.

1. I feel comfortable recognizing the contributions of the people I lead to my leaders
2. I feel threatened by the success of the people I lead
3. I am comfortable sharing credits with my team members when it is due
4. By sharing credits, the people I lead may end up being more successful than me
5. I enable the people I lead in every way possible
6. I believe it is important for me to keep my advantage over my reports by withholding information and skills.
7. The scope of my growth extends beyond my current function or organization
8. If I let my immediate circle be successful, I will become irrelevant in my organization.

Give yourself a +1 score for each Yes for
questions 1, 3, 5, 7.
Give yourself a -1 score for each Yes for
question 2, 4, 6, 8.
Score Interpretation: Positive scores indicate an abundance
of thinking. Negative scores indicate that you may need to
work on abundance thinking in your leadership.

Tips for practicing abundance thinking

Here are some ideas to put abundance thinking into practice in the
workplace:

- Remind yourself that there is plenty to go around, even if
  it seems otherwise
- Make a habit of honestly complimenting people
- Share knowledge and skills freely, but also practice bound-
  aries
- Welcome competition, and keep a learning mindset
- Think big and be thankful
- Appreciate people who are abundant with their time and
  resources

To expand your own capacity for abundance, you could experiment with selfless acts of giving. Try this little experiment.

**Today at work, do the most abundant act or give the most
abundant gift you can, but do it anonymously. What did you
learn from being anonymously selfless?**

_____

_____

_____

_____

_____

_____

_____

_____

_____
_____
_____
_____
_____
_____
_____
_____

MY KEY TAKEAWAYS FROM THIS CHAPTER

_____
_____
_____
_____
_____
_____
_____
_____
_____
_____
_____
_____

Mindfulness

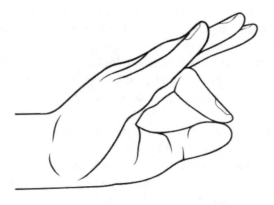

The Monkey Mind

A man retreated to a forest to meditate and find enlightenment. He found a quiet spot by a river, sat down, closed his eyes, and began to meditate. All was well through the evening and night. The next morning, his meditation was disturbed by the sound of anklet bells. He opened his eyes and saw a beautiful village girl fetching water from the river. For a while, he forgot his meditation and began admiring this girl- her physical appearance, the subtle perfume of her jasmine flowers, and the rhythm of her anklet bells as she walked. This girl was all his mind could think about throughout the day. In the evening, he gathered his thoughts and vowed not to let his mind be distracted again. He deduced that if he did not see the girl, he would not think about her. So the next morning, he woke up early and tied a cloth around his eyes and began to meditate. But when the girl came, the sound of her anklet bells distracted him, and again, all he could think of through the day was her. The following morning he not only covered up his eyes, but he also stuffed his ears with cotton wool. But when the girl came, even though he could not see her or hear her, her perfume broke his meditation.

Having lost yet another day to the girl, the next morning, the man wrapped his eyes, stuffed his ears, and covered his nose with multiple layers of linen cloth. He sat in his place, quite sure that the girl could no longer disturb his meditation. But as he sat, all his mind could do was wonder about the girl: 'Is she here now? What color are her clothes today? Is she looking at me? Laughing at me?' As his thoughts heaved and pushed against his helpless mind, he realized this: no cloth, linen, or cotton wool could tie down his mind.

Our minds are not designed to stay still. When we are triggered, the amygdala, the fear center of our brain, lights up. The amygdala sends information to the prefrontal cortex to process the threat. The prefrontal cortex is the control panel of the brain. This is the place where higher-order functions, decision-making, self-awareness, goal setting, planning, etc. happen. The prefrontal cortex, when it receives alarm signals from the amygdala, can set off a worry-loop. A worry-loop is where the prefrontal cortex responds to an alarm with projections of all the things that can potentially go wrong[10]. This magnifies the alarm signal, and a feedback cycle of fear and worry is created. If this cycle is not blocked, the persistent and repetitive worry (aka rumination) can cause depression, insomnia, and a host of other mental and physical issues.

How do we interrupt the cycle of worry and rumination?

There is a saying that the human mind is like a drunken monkey, stung by a scorpion and hanging from a tree. One of the first things shifts is to realize how monkey-like our minds are. Let's try an experiment.

Close your eyes, and for the next two minutes, think of anything *except a hippopotamus. Anything is fine, as long as it is not a hippopotamus*.

How did it go?

Were you able to block the hippo from your mind?

Tibetan Buddhist teacher **Mingyur Rinpoche** shares that the best way to work with a monkey mind is to treat it as you would a real monkey. You cannot order a monkey to stay still and expect it to do so. Instead, you could try and keep him busy. Perhaps giving the monkey a banana will stop him from being so jumpy. In the same way, you cannot order your mind to not think of anything and expect compliance. You could instead engage your monkey mind in an activity. For example, you could ask your mind to observe your breath and bring back your attention to the breath if you catch it wandering away.

Mindfulness tools

This gentle process of directing the mind to breath is an effective form of mindfulness meditation. Breath is a great focal point for mindfulness meditation. Breath is always there. Breath is essentially inert (i.e., it does not trigger emotions). We have control over how we pace our breath. By pacing our breath to exhale longer, we can willfully reduce the fight or flight response and activate vagal functions.

But there are other things we can use as focal points. For example, we could place our attention on sensations- doing a scan of our body from head to toe- noticing how the body feels in the moment.

Or we could chant a particular sound, any sound that is special for us, over and over.

The ability to turn attention to breath or body sensations at the time of trigger is a skill that is strengthened with practice. With breathing, for example, multiple methods have been suggested, each varying in the time of the duration of inhaling-holding-exhaling. All of the breathing methods try to extend the exhale time to activate the vagal response. One of the more popular methods is **the 4-7-8 breathing pattern**[11] by **Dr. Andrew Weil** based on a yogic style called Pranayama. In this method, you inhale for 4 seconds, hold your breath for 7 and then exhale for 8 seconds through your mouth.

In certain situations, and for some of us, it is not easy to turn our attention to the breath. So we give the monkey mind a different task. We ask it to observe and imagine. We ask our minds to simply become curious and observe. It is not easy to observe and not be judgmental about it. There are plenty of triggers that can come up with observing reality. But if you decide to constrain your mind just to be the observer and not the reactor, then challenges flow by you like a river. That simple decision of saying, 'I am not going to control the flow of this reality. I am simply going to look at my reality as it is. I am going to watch this like a movie' is an act of power. By giving up control, you gain control. After all, if a situation forces you to react, it has control over you. If you say, 'No, thank you. Today I am just going to watch' the situation loses power.

Sometimes, I sit and imagine that life is a river flowing by me. It will flow if I am there and if I am not there. While my reactions make me, me, I do not have to react all the time. I can react little and impact more.

I suffer
I watch me suffer
This suffering
- it comes and it goes
I see a flower
My suffering fades
The flower wilts
The fruit happens
Seasons pass
Change changes
I observe
I am only the observer

A beautiful foundation of mindful observation is keeping open the 'beginner's mind'. The beginner's mind is essentially the skill to look at any given experience with a sense of wonderment and awe, just as we would if we were looking at them for the very first time, without a sense of entitlement or judgment. The beginners' mindset is what makes so many of our childhood memories so poignant. A popular experience tool to open up the beginner's mind is the **Raisin exercise**.

Imagine you are an alien visiting earth. You encounter a raisin. You have no idea what it is, but you are filled with a deep curiosity to learn about it. What would you do? Perhaps you would take a close look at it, admire its shriveled frame, wonder if it is alive. Perhaps you would then venture to talk to it, touch it, smell it. Perhaps you would then surmise that it is edible. So with trepidation, you might lick it, put it on your tongue, feel its textures, and then bite into it, and experience its delicious goodness.

If we are used to eating raising by the mouthful, it might come as a shock that there is so much magic in a single raisin. Everything is magical if only we choose to see the magic. As Albert Einstein wrote, *"There are only two ways to live your life. One is as though nothing is a miracle. The other is as though everything is a miracle."*

Perspective-taking is another powerful mindfulness exercise. We will take a more in-depth look at perspectives when we dissect big-picture thinking. But the ability to observe and see through the eyes of another is again a skill that becomes easier with practice. Let's say a colleague slights me. Before any conversation happens, I sit down and imagine how the world looks like through the other person's eyes. I do this, not to justify what they do, but so that I can bring myself to a place of centeredness. I have personally experienced swelling waves of anger dissolve into trickling streams of annoyance by practicing the art of observing and perspective-taking.

An interesting experiment to try in your team-building meeting is the *perspective dyad*. In this exercise, people pair up, and after setting the tone for shared respect and intent, one person shares an experience, while the other listens actively without verbal interruption. Then the roles shift, and the listener is now the speaker, mirroring a similar experience from his/her own life, while the other listens intently. For example, the topic for perspective dyad in a team-building meeting could be 'What was your experience on the first day of your working here?'

The dyad experience ends with thanking each other genuinely for sharing. Often there is newfound respect that people say has been created because of the exercise.

Another category of mindfulness practice involves digging into our own pro-social inclinations to disrupt the worry loop. As a compassion teacher, this is something I lean on heavily. A time tested method is the Metta Practice of loving-kindness meditation.

Metta

Metta is an ancient eastern practice that invites us to recognize our own unlimited capacity for compassion for ourselves and for the world around us. The practice starts with offering kind wishes for ourselves. We then offer blessings to someone we love. Following this, as a recognition of the universality of the need for compassion, we offer our loving-kindness to a stranger. Then, as an act of breaking past our judgments and fears, we extend compassionate wishes to a person who has hurt or challenged us in some way. As a lotus flower opens up into multiple layers, we continue to expand our loving-kindness to the world and all its beings. The vital aspect of Metta is the authenticity of wishing. As we hold the person we want to bless in our hearts, we remember our common humanity, that all of us desire for love, happiness, and kindness. It sometimes helps to imagine that the recipient of our blessings and wishes is sitting with us, either next to us or across us at a table. This visualization can add an element of intimacy to the Metta process. Besides being a time tested tool for happiness, the value of Metta practices has been validated by contemporary science. Multiple studies have demonstrated that the volume of the grey matter in our brain increases with the practice of loving-kindness meditation. Barbara Fredrickson and colleagues in a 2008 paper showed that a 7-week practice of loving-kindness meditation increases self-reported scores feeling of well-being and positive affect[12]. (reference)

Let us do a short Metta exercise

Please make sure you are in a safe, comfortable place when you do this meditation. It is helpful if someone can guide you through this process. Give yourself the mental permission to stay uninterrupted by your responsibilities. This is a time for self-nourishment, and you deserve it.

When you are comfortable close your eyes. Sit with your spine erect if possible, but making sure you are not strained.

Scan your body, starting with your toes and gently moving your awareness all the way to the top of your head. Notice the places in your body where you are feeling tense. Is your shoulder tight? Are your hands clenched? Are your toes curled inward? How does the place of contact between your feet and the ground feel?

Let's start by taking a few deep breaths to relax your body.

Allow your breath to come back to its normal pattern.

Imagine you are sitting at a table on a beautiful day. Everything is perfect. The air, the smells, the colors… you become aware that you are living in a beautiful, abundant world. A sense of deep gratitude and happiness envelops you. You notice that you deserve all the beauty and joy that life has given you. You are a beautiful and unique part of this universe. You deserve love and happiness.

As a way of emphasizing this beauty and happiness, I invite you to repeat these words of kindness for yourself:

May I be free from danger and anxiety

May I be loved

May I be happy

May I be at ease

At this table, someone you love has joined you. This person or being loves you unconditionally. You too love them and care for them. Like you, they also deserve to share the beauty and joy of this incredible life journey.

I invite you to wish this person or being you love these blessings of loving-kindness:

May they be free from danger and anxiety

May they be loved

May they be happy

May they be at ease

There is still room at your table for more. I invite you to welcome a stranger to your table. This is a person you do not know well. Perhaps it is the barista who serves you coffee in the mornings. Or the person who lives a few houses down, who you meet every day but never connected with. Remember that this person, like you, wants to be happy and loved. And in wishing them well, your love only expands and grows.

I invite you to wish this person or being you love these blessings of loving-kindness:

May they be free from danger and anxiety

May they be loved

May they be happy

May they be at ease

I now invite you to consider inviting to your table a person who has hurt or slighted you. You may feel uncomfortable inviting this person to sit with you, but this person, like you, is looking for love, happiness, success in his or her world in his or her own way. This person is someone's child, someone's parent, someone's friend. They like you, need the things you crave for, including love and happiness.

In a spirit of abundance, you choose to give this person your blessings of loving-kindness:

May they be free from danger and anxiety

May they be loved

May they be happy

May they be at ease

I invite you to consider that all the beauty around you is not yours alone. This beauty and has been around long before you and will continue long after you. That you are sharing this moment with the world and all its amazement is a gift to be truly thankful for.

I invite you to express your gratitude to the world and all its creatures, including you with these wishes:

May we all be free from danger and anxiety

May we be loved

May we be happy

May we all be at ease

I invite you to bring your awareness to your body and your breathing again. Has anything shifted in the past few minutes?

Take a few deep breaths, paying attention to the beauty of life-giving air going in and coming out.

When you are ready, I welcome you to open your eyes and return to this reality.

There is no one way to practice Metta.

Metta Meditation can be practiced as a sitting meditation or as an on-the-go practice. Once you have created a ritual of blessing people with your loving kindness, you could try experimenting it as an ongoing practice throughout the day. For example, you could walk into a room full of people, and in silence, wish everyone present there unconditional love and happiness. You could be preparing for a difficult conversation with a colleague or client, and you could realize that beyond the business facade is a human being deserving of love and wish them loving kindness. Someone could cut you off in traffic, and instead of cursing, you could choose to bless them with simple wishes that come from an authentic place of wishing people well:

May we all be free from danger and anxiety

May we be loved

May we be happy

May we be at ease

These blessings take only a few seconds of our time, but the transformations they bring are incredible.

In 'Man's Search for Meaning' Viktor Frankl makes a powerful observation. He says, *'Between stimulus and response there is a space. In that space is our power to choose our response. In our response lies our growth and our freedom.'*

When we are triggered, we can choose whether to propagate the worry-loop or stop it. With mindfulness practices, since we are not paying attention to the worry, but directing our attention to an inert reality, or taking on perspectives of others or digging into our personal wells of compassion, we are deflating the power of worry. We discussed the worry loop between the amygdala and the prefrontal cortex. Mindfulness meditation breaks the loop. In fact, it has been shown that meditation can reduce the size of the amygdala. This means that we are not reactive. We choose to disallow situations that trigger us. By being mindful, we have created a space between the stimulus and the response. And in that space, we can make compassionate choices. This is where mindfulness becomes a pillar of compassion.

WHY MINDFULNESS MATTERS

"people spend nearly half their time (46.7%) thinking about something other than what they are actually doing...reminiscing, thinking ahead or daydreaming tends to make people more miserable, even when they are thinking about something pleasant."- Killingsworth and Gilbert[13]

There has been a dramatic increase in interest in mindfulness research in the past two decades. According to statistics from the American Mindfulness Research Association in the year 2000, there were only ten mindfulness journal publications. By 2016, there were 690 publications[14]. There is a great deal of research backing what we always anecdotally believed to be true. Mindfulness can fundamentally rewire our brains and heal our bodies, and in the workplace, avoid conflict and improve productivity

Mindfulness in Action

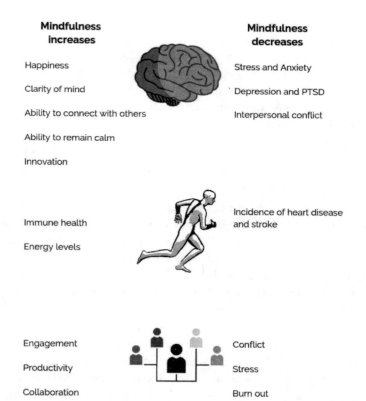

Mindfulness increases

Happiness

Clarity of mind

Ability to connect with others

Ability to remain calm

Innovation

Immune health

Energy levels

Engagement

Productivity

Collaboration

Mindfulness decreases

Stress and Anxiety

Depression and PTSD

Interpersonal conflict

Incidence of heart disease and stroke

Conflict

Stress

Burn out

COMPASSION AND MINDFULNESS

Mindfulness also facilitates all the other compassion pillars because it is all about rewiring the brain in a certain intentional way. It is easier for a mindful mind to become aware of the challenges it is experiencing and therefore respond with compassion. Being mindful increases the time and space for making compassionate choices when we are triggered. If we practice Metta mindfulness as a routine, we create positive bonds with our colleagues at work. When challenges do show up, the positive relationship frameworks that we create in our minds through Metta meditation will help us reframe issues and resolve with more human success. Perspective-taking, as we will see in big-picture thinking, can be a powerful tool that helps work through situations we have little control of. Mindful choices help create a sound mental foundation for being appropriately vulnerable with people, as also with taking time to appreciate our shared existence and uniqueness.

Rachel Weissman, Interaction Designer at Google, shares her experience about how practicing mindfulness changed her life.

"While living and working in Chicago, I experienced consistent migraines, anxiety, and depression. In an attempt to relieve my pain and suffering, I began using an app to form a simple meditation practice. A couple of years after living in Chicago, I accepted an opportunity with Salesforce in San Francisco as a Product Designer. My job was to create the best value and experience to a target audience. On a micro-level, this consisted of day-to-day creation, iteration, and collaboration. With an increased scope of work and responsibility in this role, I knew it was vital to develop a resilient and optimistic mental state.

Looking to evolve my meditation practice upon moving to San Francisco, I enrolled in a Transcendental Meditation (TM) course. My daily TM practice consisted of one twenty-minute sit in the morning, and a second twenty-minute sit in the afternoon. This meant that Monday through Friday I had to carve out time to meditate at work. Because I was committed to forming this habit, I added a 2 pm daily meeting to my work calendar titled "Meditate." This small act of creating space for myself became the springboard for weaving self-compassion into my life.

As this daily practice progressed, I was not only affected immediately after my sit, but my overall mindset and behavior began to change. Meditating made me feel clear-headed and energized. When approaching problems and situations at work, I was more present, aware, and balanced. I also started to be more kind to myself, which resulted in acting more kind to others. This transformation made me much more effective when collaborating with my teammates, partners, and stakeholders.

Since expanding my meditation practice, I have learned how to exercise mindful self-compassion, which further evolved my approach to my professional life. I realized that how I treat and connect with others is a pure reflection of how I treat and connect with myself. By cultivating a present awareness of lovingkindness, I could shatter any limiting beliefs I had towards myself, thus allowing me to grow professionally in ways I may not have believed were possible. **"**

MINDFULNESS-ON-THE-GO

Since mindfulness helps us navigate our current challenges without the pinpricks of the past or the anxieties of the future, we can focus more effectively on the tasks at hand, and allow ourselves to become more productive and engaged. But like all good things, to harness its effect on our physical, mental, and social well being, we must create habits out of mindfulness practices.

As we discussed, there are several different types of mindfulness practices. If mindfulness meditation is not already a part of your everyday living, I would urge you to consider experimenting with different kinds of mindfulness to figure out which is most meaningful for you.

One of the points I want to emphasize here is that mindfulness practices do not have to be sitting exercises. As we go through the day, we have multiple opportunities to practice mindfulness. For example, as we discussed with Metta mindfulness, we could walk into a meeting, and use that as an opportunity to wish everyone Metta wishes.

Or we could take a deliberate moment to pause to breathe and center before a meeting. A friend of mine, a doctor who works in ER medicine in a large hospital system, makes it a practice to pause outside her patient's rooms for a full minute before walking in, to focus on her breathing and center herself. Ever since she has created this habit for herself, she reports that she feels less burnt out and anxious. Her patients love her even more because she is able to give her full presence to them.

Here is an example of a mindful pause exercise to pepper throughout your day. It literally only takes a minute.

- Position yourself comfortably. Close your eyes if that's possible. Take a few long deep breaths, making sure that your exhalation time is longer than inhalation time.
- Remind yourself that you have a choice to be compassionate, no matter what the situation.
- Feel gratitude for your ability to choose your mindset, as you return to your task at hand.

Another mindfulness-on-the-go exercise is to perform ordinary activities with extraordinary deliberation. A friend of mine, a manager in a software company, suffered from chronic shoulder pain issues. Even though she did not realize it, her naturally anxious personality and sticky mindset were expressing as psychosomatic issues. When we discussed the issues, I suggested that she make an effort to calm her mind as a way of working with her physical ailments. She was initially skeptical but decided to give an earnest try anyway. We decided that we would start with coffee. Instead of the rushed gulps, she was used to, while staring at the computer; she began to make every coffee break an opportunity for mindfulness and grounding. She started by using her non-dominant hand to pick up the coffee mug, began to savor every sip, and utilizing the quietness to think prosocial thoughts. Coffee time became about gratitude, letting go, forgiveness. In two months, she reported becoming calmer and happier than she had been in a very long time. This is the power of the mind, and this is the power of mindfulness.

Access to mindful tools is not a challenge in our current world of technology. There are plenty of apps and online resources that offer mindfulness meditations. Teachers of the masters are at our fingertips to access when we want to. The real challenge is being consistent with training once we have started the effort. This desire can come from no one but us. Hopefully, this discussion has been an invitation to experiment with different mindfulness practices, to adopt mindfulness as part of your daily routine going forward. And if it impacts you meaningfully, share those tools with others in your life, including those in your workplace.

MINDFULNESS IN THE WORKPLACE

Here are some ideas to make mindfulness practices a part of your workday:

- Mindfulness can be a moment-by-moment way of living and being. Setting intentions to be mindful as a part of your waking up practices can make the practice tangible.
- Try to do mundane things with deliberation. A trip to the coffee machine can be an act of mindful centering.
- Break a routine. For example, before you drink your coffee, take time to sniff it, savor it, and make it a gratitude moment.
- Ban your electronics from human conversations. Try and approach every person with a sense of curiosity and wonderment which is the beginner's mindset
- Remember that your choices define your uniqueness. You can choose to be reactive or proactive.
- Create moments of silence throughout your day, and honor it as non-negotiable time.
- Practice the one-minute mindful pause exercise before difficult conversations
- If possible, engage in a sitting meditation practice routine. This can help bolster your on-the-go mindfulness efforts at work.
- When you are reacting to something challenging, pause to observe your emotions. Simply label the feelings as they come and go. Remember that, as an observer, you cannot intervene.
- Practice Metta meditation regularly/as much as possible. It can really shift the way how you react to stressful situations.

ENCOURAGING MINDFULNESS AS A LEADER

As we practice mindfulness, we show up with that much better presence because of how we interact with the world around us. It would then be natural, in the spirit of compassion, to encourage others to experience the same goodness. If your role in your organization gives you any sphere of influence, it is an opportunity to encourage others to become mindful and give them the tools and skills to become mindful. This is not easy in some environments. But mindfulness is becoming a standard workplace verb, that the resistance is not likely to be untenable with the right approach.

Consider the story of Birju, who made a choice of mind(fulness) over matter.

Birju Pandya, Social Impact Investor

"A few years ago, I was working in an investment fund. On my one year review, the principal of my investment fund called me to his office and said, 'Birju, you have done well. What do you want?' That is a godfather offer if you work in an investment firm. I did not know what to ask. I paused for a while; then I said, 'I know what I want. Every time before we have a team meeting, I want us to spend a minute in silence' My boss stared at me for what seemed like a very long time, and said 'No.' We talked some more, and he offered to consider my request. I guess he must have considered what else I could have asked, so the next day he agreed. I had come prepared with my singing bowl, and we started meeting with a minute of silence. In the four years since, the transformation that has happened in my organization is nothing short of astounding.

The one minute of silence became two, extended to five minutes before some meetings, and 30 minutes of silence once a week. And then it became even deeper. As a team we began experimenting with random acts of kindness. We would go to restaurants, pick a random table to pay for and reflect on it as a team. This soon evolved into a practice and we were doing 21--days of gratitude and 21--days of mindfulness, and multi-day events where investment bankers are talking about how to bring their services in line with the compassion that we were practicing. And so now we have an investment firm, perhaps the only investment firm, where taking a loan means a commitment to take on daily actions for a 21-day kindness challenge. **"**

Here are some ideas you can try to encourage others in your team to practice mindfulness:

- Create a mindfulness experience. Invite a mindfulness teacher for lunch and learn. Experience can break down the walls of resistance in incredible ways.

- Create a mindfulness club with other people in your organization. Identify others in your organization who are passionate about creating mindful workplaces and team up with them. Create a fun project bringing people together on a mindfulness event.

- Collect numbers. Get feedback from attendees of your mindfulness programs. When you have reasonable numbers, it may be easier to receive support from management to make your offering available throughout your company.

- Most importantly, inspire by example. When your team members and employees see a successful leader who is calm and mindful, they would want to emulate you. That is how changes are made, one monkey mind at a time.

- Create a collective commitment to start any team/group meetings with one minute of silence.

- Teach the concept of mindful pause. Encourage the practice of mindfully pausing before difficult conversations. Later in a group meeting, encourage people to share specific incidents that happened or perspectives that shifted by the practice of pausing mindfully.

What are some steps I can take as an influencer in my current job setting to promote mindfulness?

_____

_____

_____

_____

_____

_____

_____

_____

_____

_____

_____

_____

_____

_____

MY KEY TAKEAWAYS FROM THIS CHAPTER

_____

_____

_____

_____

_____

_____

_____

_____

_____

_____

_____

_____

Embracing Oneness

"We are one. Everything in the universe is within you. Ask all from yourself." - **Rumi**

Seeing self in others

One of the goals of the compassion journey is to embrace the universality of our existence. This is a realization that leads us to a higher plane of thinking and action. All of us, irrespective of how we look and act, carry the same fundamental aspirations to be happy, to live with purpose, and be loved. This involves letting go of a lifetime of conditioning and fear of the 'other'. Most of the calamities created by humans stem from a fundamental inability to see Self in others. Most of the strife that happens in workplaces also happens when people forget that they are no different from the people who are sharing this workplace journey with them.

Black and white are easier to work with than shades of gray. It is easy to bin people as our kind and not-our-kind. When we classify someone as our kind, it is easier to work with them. And when we see someone is not our kind, it is easier to deny them compassion. The people who manipulate others know how to work this to their advantage. The common narrative for these people is creating a fear of others by drumming up scarcity thinking. Throughout history, this is how wars have been instigated and lives lost. But even amid the persistent narrative of others vs. us, there is a part of us that knows that we are all one. As the spiritual thinker, **Eknath Easwaran** pointed out, *'My real Self is not different from yours or anyone else's. If we want to live in the joy that increases with time, if we want to live in true freedom independent of circumstances, then we must strive to realize that even if there are four people in our family or forty at our place of work, there is only one Self.'*

Compassion, in this case, is holding our truth against popular narratives of us vs. them, knowing that those who create that narrative are either selfish or misguided.

Extreme events can make us embrace our oneness or shatter and disperse.

When terrorists attacked America on September 11th, 2001, I was a graduate student in New Orleans. Soon after the attack, a fellow graduate student, a person of Islamic faith from Egypt, had to rush home because someone had shot a firearm through his window. His wife, who was pregnant and home at the time was fortunately not hurt, but she was shaken to the core. A few days later, another friend, from India, was walking home late, when he was accosted by a group of racially triggered men who beat him up badly. My friend ended up in the hospital, and he too, was left shaken and disillusioned.

Fast forward four years, my wife, and I were expecting our first baby when hurricane Katrina struck New Orleans. We had left two days before the hurricane landed, so we did not face the impact of the damage, but we ended up in Shreveport in northern

Louisiana, with a suitcase of clothes and nothing else. We had left behind everything we had put together for our baby. But in Shreveport, as I know was true in the rest of America at that time, there was so much compassion for people like us who had left New Orleans. A Caucasian family (we are from India) invited us to live in their home. Race did not matter. On the day our baby was born, the local church had a baby shower. When we came home from the hospital to our host's home, there was a huge table piled up high with gifts for the newborn. This was everything we needed, and more. What was most moving was a ziplock bag full of quarters and dollar notes and a little note that said, 'God bless the new baby'. This was from three young children, 7, 11 and 13 years old- who had sold lemonade to collect funds for a child that they would never meet!

There is a story of a Native American boy who asks his grandfather, 'There are two wolves fighting in my heart. One is violent and cruel. The other is kind and loving. Which wolf will win?' To which his grandfather replies, 'The wolf that you feed is the wolf that will win.'

Identities and Connection

As a cancer scientist, I have been privy to the extraordinary miracles of human life. Every animal cell is a masterpiece of divinity. There are so many events that work in perfect clockwork to support this unknown force we call life. Race, wealth, nationality, religion, external preferences, and identities appear ridiculously shallow when you have seen the miraculous machinations of cells firsthand. At that level, it becomes very easy to lose identities.

This idea of identities that we hold on to so tightly is a fickle thing. All I need to do is lose a small section of my brain, and I am no longer Immanual. Another section of my brain removed, and I am only a vegetable. Yet another section lost, and I am no longer alive. This is true for every human being I will meet. We all have to go through the motions of life - when the clock turns, we will take help from whichever quarter it comes from, and all our tribal preferences dissipate to the wind.

The other thing to realize is that we are all connected. Connection is the fundamental law of nature. One of the greatest minds of the 20th century, **Nikolai Tesla** said this: *"If you want to find the secrets of the universe, think in terms of energy, frequency, and vibration."* At the quantum level, we are governed by a complexity that makes the separation of individuals obsolete. **Albert Einstein** said, *"A human being is a part of the whole called by us universe, a part limited in time and space. He experiences himself, his thoughts and feelings as something separated from the rest, a kind of optical delusion of his consciousness. This delusion is a kind of prison for us, restricting us to our personal desires and to affection for a few persons nearest to us. Our task must be to free ourselves from this prison by widening our circle of compassion to embrace all living creatures and the whole of nature in its beauty."*

Connection is one of our fundamental needs. Animal cell culture is the art of growing cells on special plates with media containing nutrients. To grow cells in these plates, we seed the plates containing growth media with cells. Under the right conditions, the cells take in nutrients, happily divide and grow. When there are too many cells in a plate, there is not enough space and there is competition for nutrients. This is expected. So one would think, a single cell in a plate of nutrients and space would thrive because there is no competition. But here is the thing: single cells fare very poorly. This is because they need a community of cells to send them growth signals and support their survival.

In the same way that we use the internet to connect with other people, trees growing in forests have an underground network made of fungi. Through this network, trees share nutrients, minerals, and even warning signals when there is a threat. But they also use this wood wide web for plant doses of 'compassion'. For example, when Paper-birch trees lose their leaves in winter and cannot produce their own food, Douglas-fir trees provide them with sugar through the fungal network. In summer, when paper birch trees are thriving, they send sugars to young Douglas fir trees growing in their shade[15].

There is a beautiful advertisement from TV2 Denmark about stepping out of boxes[16]. In this ad, people from a diverse collection of backgrounds are brought together into a room with boxes drawn on the floor. People initially self-identify the boxes they belong do: the rich, those just getting by, people from cities vs. those from the countryside and so on. The moderator then asks a series of questions (who of you have been bullied, or who was a bully, or who has experienced the loss of a loved one, or sexual preferences and such) and participants who feel it applies to them come forward to stand in those boxes and then return to their original boxes. As the questions roll, and people of different persuasions come forward to center stage, it becomes clear that our collective human experiences are not defined by the boxes we choose to place ourselves in.

An anthropologist in Africa placed a basket of fruits near a tree and told a group of kids that whoever could run to the tree first would get all the fruits. Instead of a mad race to get to the fruits, the group of children held hands and walked to the tree. There they all sat and enjoyed the fruits together. When pointed out that if they had actually raced, one of them could have had it all, they simply answered **"Ubuntu"**.

Ubuntu is a Xhosa word that means, *'I am because we are.'*

Desmond Tutu, who won the Nobel Peace Prize for his anti-apartheid activism, said this about Ubuntu, *"It is the essence of being human. It speaks of the fact that my humanity is caught up and is inextricably bound up in yours. I am human because I belong. It speaks about wholeness; it speaks about compassion. A person with Ubuntu is welcoming, hospitable, warm and generous, willing to share. Such people are open and available to others, willing to be vulnerable, affirming of others, do not feel threatened that others are able and good, for they have a proper self-assurance that comes from knowing that they belong in a greater whole. They know that they are diminished when others are humiliated, diminished when others are oppressed, diminished when others are treated as if they were less than who they are. The quality of Ubuntu gives people resilience, enabling them to survive and emerge still human despite all efforts to dehumanize them."*

As we reflect more and more on our commonalities and connections, it becomes easier to lift this illusion of non-belonging.

The more adept we become at looking past our separations, the easier it is to practice compassion universally.

Oneness in workplaces

The opposite of Oneness is neither uniqueness nor difference. It is *non-belonging*. Leaning into our shared humanity or dissecting into our differences comes down to choice.

We are working in increasingly diverse workplaces. We are traveling more and interacting more with people who look and think differently from us. We cannot afford to lug around our biases in this diverse landscape. When people are caught up in non-belonging, the harmony of the company is affected. Non-belonging mindset affects collaboration and cooperation among individuals and teams. Non-belonging hurts psychological safety. It also causes nepotism, favoring their own for personal progress, and sacrificing their broader organizational goals. Seeing others as not belonging to their work tribe makes it justifiable for some to be discompassionate to others.

The greatest tragedy of the non-belonging mindset is loneliness. Loneliness is one of the most painful experiences of human existence. There is research showing that loneliness is just as lethal as smoking 15 cigarettes a day[16]. Loneliness reduces immunity and increases the risk of heart disease. When we feel excluded from our communal setting because we do not look and feel like them, we lose our desire to contribute actively in our roles.

When we embrace Oneness, we create a culture built on sharing and respect. With inclusion and diversity, there is growth. When the whole workplace becomes 'my tribe', we feel propelled to contribute and engage more effectively. We would feel less inclined to bully anyone who is our own kind.

Knowledge is the enemy of non-belonging. The first step to embrace Oneness is to know and accept that we are all made of the same fabric. To break past notions of non-belonging and embrace Oneness, we need to have the courage to face our biases. Bias can happen over race, age, gender, physical abilities, faith, sexual orientation, weight, and many other characteristics.

To face our biases is to face our fears. We are evolved to think that anyone who looks or acts differently from us is competing for our resources, and is, therefore, a threat. But when we subscribe to abundance and accept that we have the power to break through the scarcity circle, our biases disappear. This is why Oneness as a compassion pillar is linked tightly with the Abundance mindset. And sometimes, our biases are not obvious. They are small writhing tentacles of distrust wriggling under the surface. When suffering happens, the biases shoot up to the surface. But if we take a naked, honest look at what our biases are, our biases crumble. Remember the scene from Harry Potter where Harry and his friends use the 'riddikulus' spell to fight Boggarts? In the story, Boggarts are shape-shifting beings that take on the form of a person's worst fears. The riddikulus spell turns the boggart into a form that is amusing and non-threatening. Our oneness spell can work magic on the illusion of separation and dissipate fears.

Working with biases is not that easy in real life, because we are not always aware of our biases. These are our *unconscious biases* also called implicit biases. We learn early to stereotype people and create certain limiting beliefs about them. One of the ways to fight unconscious biases is to sit with ourselves and ask some difficult questions.

Try this little exercise for one or two people in your workplace who you find it difficult to identify as your tribe. Reflect on the non-belonging stories you carry about them. What would it take for you to see them as part of 'your' tribe?

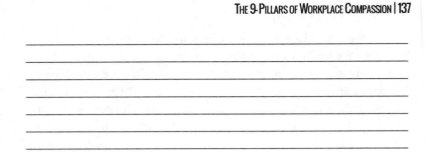

Oneness is embracing Diversity, Equity and Inclusion (DEI)

Diversity in the organizational context is the representation of people from multiple backgrounds- races, genders, nationalities, sexual orièntations, etc. Building diversity is bringing people from a range of backgrounds to the system. The intention of building diversity in a system helps ameliorate a paucity of representation of a particular group of people in the company or society. A diverse environment allows for the creation of new perspectives and ideas that would be otherwise absent in a homogeneous setting.

Now that a diverse physical environment with multiple representations of people has been created, all these diverse people must feel that they belong to the group. They must feel welcomed, accepted, safe, and valued. This is what inclusion is about. While creating diversity is the physical act of creating a heterogeneous environment, being inclusive is capitalizing on diversity for positive human and business outcomes. Inclusion focuses on the human experience.

Equity is a yardstick to help practice fairness in inclusion. Equity is often confused with equality. While equality says equal opportunities for all, equity takes into consideration that real fairness involves consideration of people's historical disadvantages and providing additional resources to enable them to operate at the same level as the rest of the team. Practicing equity requires awareness and acceptance of the realities of social marginalization, and taking a corrective stance to address disadvantages.

Consider a simplistic example to illustrate DEI in workplaces.

A trading company XYZ in Wall Street has historically had an all-white, male employee roster, except for receptionists and administrative assistants. The new CEO of the company is committed to improving the DEI of the company. He works with his hiring managers and creates a requirement that in the next several years, the male-female gender disparity in the company will be addressed. The hiring managers step into action. A new trader, a female, is hired by the company with plans to hire more females in the coming months. XYZ Company is increasing its diversity.

Bur Sandra, the new hire, realizes that XYZ is not ready for her. On the trading floor, she feels that her colleagues discount her readily. There are many condescending behaviors- she feels her intellect and value are being undermined by a group that is not accustomed to working with women. Her male colleagues pass sexist jokes, which Sandra feels are inappropriate. After she pointed this out a couple of times, her colleagues become wary of her presence. Sometimes they stop conversations midway when they notice she is around. Sandra feels neither wanted nor valued. She talks about this to her CEO. Her CEO realizes that while none of her colleagues may be necessarily mean, they are just not skilled in dealing with a coworker of a different gender. He hires a DEI trainer who assesses the situation and works with the team to create an environment where Sandra and all other incoming female colleagues will be treated in ways they will feel valued and can contribute successfully. XYZ's employees realize the implicit biases they have been operating with and decide to work on it. Slowly but steadily, XYZ company achieves what it set out to do in terms of diversity and inclusion. The company, in turn, has noticed a significant jump in its business outcomes- with the team taking non-traditional approaches to gain clients that were not considered earlier. Among the new recruits in XYZ are two new mothers. To accommodate their needs, XYZ has created a lactation room for the young mothers and also created a certain level of flexibility in their attendance to meetings as needed. This allows for the young mothers to perform their duties in an environment that is fair to their needs.

Let us look at a real-life example of DEI in action:

Joe Hansen
Transformational Change Consultant, Shell

"I was always quite reluctant to talk about being dyslexic. Dyslexia is an interesting condition. It puts me at an advantage in certain scenarios and at a disadvantage in others. For example, dyslexic people may sometimes struggle in reading, time management and usually in minor and simple ways, but can excel in communication, intuition, and both creative and strategic tasks. As my thought process works a little differently, I'm noted for providing creative themes and ideas from a different perspective. Einstein is a perfect example of this, with the theory of relativity. For most people though, the stigma with dyslexics can be seen as often clumsy or unable to do the smaller things, therefore, may not be trusted with bigger things despite technological advancements minimizing most of the negatives of the double-sided condition, and that can carry a negative perception with people. The right environment can make a fundamental difference with someone who is dyslexic.

In previous companies I worked with, I was not comfortable talking about my condition. Many companies talk about diversity and inclusion but fail to deliver. In the one instance that I did mention it a past company, my revelation was met with awkward silence. Soon several of my projects were taken away from me, and I decided to leave the company. For this reason, I was hesitant to talk about my dyslexia when I joined Shell.

But I soon found that Shell was an environment that truly believed in inclusion. Shell is very large and operates globally. Diversity within the company is very real. Shell understands that, for its global workforce to operate seamlessly, they must be taught to embrace and value diversity. All employees at Shell have access to a myriad of training programs to develop diversity and inclusion skills. Thanks to this constant reinforcement, managers are empowered to work with diversity and disability with compassion.

Even though I had my trepidations about opening up about my dyslexia when I joined Shell, I found it easy to open up to my manager about my condition. My manager was a trustworthy, compassionate, and approachable person. When I spoke to her about my dyslexia, instead of silence or judgment, she responded with curiosity. She created a safe space where I could talk about the challenges and advantages of my condition without feeling judged. More importantly, her compassion extended into action. She worked with me to identify scenarios where I could thrive, instead of trying to mold me to fit into a box. Thanks to her compassion skills, I moved from technical roles into people-focused roles. I even led a diversity and inclusion program in my company recently. In my people-focused roles at Shell, I thrive now- thanks to a compassionate manager who was trained to think and act compassionately in the face of diversity, by a company that cares."

Companies that are successful with their DEI programs make sure that the diversity message is communicated effectively across the organization. As a leader, it will help to create a clear internal marketing strategy for your organization's DEI. Companies with successful DEI programs also try to get their employees actively involved in co-creating solutions. Successful leaders can help their people see diversity as an opportunity and not as a threat.

Promoting oneness in workplaces

Another way companies can get involved in promoting inclusion is by creating opportunities for people to share their cultural uniqueness in their workplaces. Some large organizations have 'cultural days' as a way to invite people from different races to share food and cultural expressions and inviting others to partake.

One of the apparent expressions of inclusion in organizations is language. Every organization has its own language. *The language of the workplace is a physical expression of its culture.* Some of that language is verbal, and some of it is not. Some companies use inclusive language. Some companies use divisive language.

Why is language important? Because people who control the language of the organization, wield power over the company culture. History has shown this to be true, repeatedly. For example, the Nazi leadership carefully framed language to mask their acts of terror. In the language of the Nazis, Sonderbehandlung ("special treatment") meant execution, and the term Endlösung ("final solution") referred to the systematic extermination and mass murder of the Jewish peoples[17]. We, with our current awareness of compassion, can deliberately create a language of inclusion and belonging.

For example, we can discourage the I's and encourage the We's, trade gender-biased for gender-neutral words (mankind to humankind), discourage culturally or politically sensitive discussions in the workplace. The challenge I see though, is that some people become so caught up in being politically correct with their language that they actually become discompassionate in the process. The important thing is to stick to the intent, which is the alleviation of suffering for everyone involved.

As a leader, you could try to experiment with promoting the oneness-culture in your team or organization. Here are some ideas:

- Be genuinely curious about the people you lead
- Allow your people to share personal stories about their culture and heritage
- Recognize their important life events
- Create opportunities for non-judgmental conversations
- Model the habit of using oneness language, 'We' 'Us' 'Together' 'Team' and encourage others to use the same in their conversations

Here are some exercises to consider to kick-start Oneness dialogs in your team meetings.

- Pair up members of your team randomly. Within each pair, members take turns sharing a life experience (for example, experiences on their first day at your company) for 2 minutes or so. The partners reciprocate by mirroring their own experience. They then reflect on their common experiences.
- This is a simple pairing exercise that can be done during team meetings. As the person leading the exercise, you could lead with the following script. "Sit comfortably facing your partner. Try to look into the person's eyes, without staring. The biggest gift you can give them right here, right now is your complete presence, without judgment.

As you look into your partner's eyes, try to remember that this person has many similarities with you. This person is someone's child, someone's parent, and someone's favorite person. This person like you is motivated by the needs of love and happiness. This person cares for someone, is loved by someone, whatever their outward presence is."

How will you promote a culture of oneness in your organization, as an employee and influencer?

_____

_____

_____

_____

_____

_____

_____

_____

_____

_____

_____

MY KEY TAKEAWAYS FROM THIS CHAPTER

_____

_____

_____

_____

_____

_____

_____

_____

_____

_____

_____

Compassionate communication

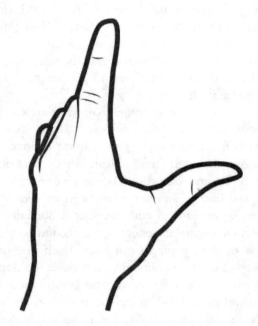

Communication is one of the most important pillars of compassionate workplaces. How we communicate, what we communicate, when we communicate is how we interface us with the world we live in. What we choose to put out into the world as a representation of our inner world- our words, our body language, our emails, and even our silence- are opportunities for alleviating suffering. Even as we experiment with compassion skills, we need to create the proper channels for compassion to flow out into the external world. It can put us in a place of great power and influence.

To communicate with compassion, we need to know others, and ourselves appreciate our differences and uniqueness, set meaningful expectations, and have tools that can help us make specific choices in the heat of the moment.

Knowing ourselves and others

Compassionate communication appreciating the uniqueness of ourselves and others we work with.

In the forecourt of the Temple of Apollo at Delphi sits an enduring aphorism attributed to the Greek God Apollo. *Gnothi Seauton*- which means, Know Thyself! What makes me, me? Why do I do the things I do? Why do I react the way I react during good times and bad times? Gnothi seauton is not easy. But this is the root of wisdom itself.

Knowing self is one thing. Knowing others is a different beast. People come in all flavors. Some flavors we can appreciate, some we do not care for. This we cannot control. What we can control is our choice to communicate with others on *our* terms of compassion. To understand others and give them compassion, we need to come in with an open mindset to appreciate their uniqueness. Even as we learn to embrace shared humanity and strive to see ourselves in others' experiences, we need to be cognizant of the uniqueness of the people in our lives. Each one of us carries a unique personality fingerprint that can never be duplicated. Each one of us carries a specific set of expectations about how we want to be seen and treated. When those expectations are not met, there is dissonance. Appreciating differences, as a key element of compassionate communication, allows people to feel valued and empowered.

- As we develop the skill of appreciating differences, we realize
- That we are connected, but people are unique. The uniqueness of people is not to be feared but seen as an opportunity for growth
- That we have to embrace our own uniqueness, not walk away from it
- That in order to truly bank on the opportunities that appreciating differences brings, we must learn to set clear expectations and communicate with clarity

The Golden Rule asks us to treat others as we treat ourselves. Noted speaker and author **Dr. Tony Alessandra** noted that the golden rule failed to appreciate the unique expectations of individuals. He proposed the *'Platinum Rule'*, which encourages us, 'to treat others as they would like to be treated.' The Platinum Rule can be a powerful element of compassionate communication.

Here is a little story (source unknown) that illustrates the importance of communicating preferences and appreciating differences:

A couple who had been married for 30 years were celebrating their wedding anniversary. The couple had a morning routine, which they had followed religiously through the many years of their marriage. It was this: Every morning, the wife would wake up and bake fresh bread. She would slice up the top portion of the bread, which she considered as the best part and set it aside for her husband. She would then eat the crusty bottom portion of the bread. In her mind, giving up the best part of the bread for her husband was an expression of love. But on this day, at the thirtieth wedding anniversary, the wife had a different idea.

'All these years I have given up the best part of the bread for my husband,' she thought. 'I deserve some of the good stuff too!'

So she sliced up the top soft part of the bread and ate it. It was delicious. Only the crusty part remained for her husband. Now that the deed was done, the wife became anxious. What would her husband feel about being given the inferior portion of the bread?

The husband came, and as always sat down for his bread. He seemed a little surprised that he had the crust today, but he ate it up.

Instead of being upset, he seemed happy.

"Thank you dear wife"' he said. "For thirty years, I wanted to eat the crust, because that is the best part of any bread. But I know you love it too, so I never asked. But today for our wedding anniversary, you have sacrificed the best part for me. Thank you!' "

Remember an experience when someone said or did something for you in a positive spirit and it ended up disappointing or hurting you. What could have been different if they had practiced the Platinum Rule?

_____

_____

_____

_____

_____

_____

_____

_____

_____

_____

_____

_____

Celebrating uniqueness

Our uniqueness is an opportunity for celebration. Dr. Ali Binazir calculates that the probability of use even existing is 1 X10^2685000. That is a ridiculously small number! Our very existence is a miracle[18]. If at all we could calculate a probabilistic number for why our personality is shaped the way it is, I believe it would be a number likely too minuscule to be meaningful. Yet, in our interactions with others, we become upset when others are different from us. Their customs and preferences irk us, their behaviors bother us, and their routines scare us. To being appreciating and celebrating our differences, we need to start from a place of fearless curiosity.

Try this simple exercise.

Think of a person you know who is very different from you (racially, culturally, behaviorally). What judgments do you subconsciously carry about this person? What are three questions you can ask that will help you understand why this person is so different from you?

_____

_____

_____

_____

_____

_____

_____

_____

_____

_____

_____

_____

_____

_____

_____

_____

_____

_____

Even as we appreciate the uniqueness of the people in our lives, we need to celebrate our own. When we learn to appreciate our own uniqueness and beauty, we become powerful in conviction. From that deep place of conviction, compassion becomes possible. One of the greatest invitations to appreciate our uniqueness and to stand tall in our strengths comes from **Marianne Willaimson** in her book, 'A Return to Love: Reflections on the Principles of A Course in Miracles'. She writes:

'Our deepest fear is not that we are inadequate. Our deepest fear is that we are powerful beyond measure. It is our light, not our darkness that most frightens us. We ask ourselves, Who am I to be brilliant, gorgeous, talented, fabulous? Actually, who are you not to be? You are a child of God. Your playing small does not serve the world. There is nothing enlightened about shrinking so that other people won't feel insecure around you. We are all meant to shine, as children do. We were born to make manifest the glory of God that is within us. It's not just in some of us; it's in everyone. And as we let our own light shine, we unconsciously give other people permission to do the same. As we are liberated from our own fear, our presence automatically liberates others.'

In a world that is becoming increasingly flat, it is imperative to be culturally sensitive. **Cultural sensitivity** is to appreciate the fact that people from different cultures may be similar or different from us, and to be able to look at their uniqueness without judgment. When I first came to the United States many years ago, I was shocked when my thesis advisor suggested I call him by his first name, because, growing up, I had learned that anything other than a Sir or Dr. So-and-so for a Professor was unacceptable. If I dined in Japan and tried to tip a waiter, I would be rude. If I dined in the US and did not tip a waiter, I would be rude. Our offices are cultural melting pots. Even smaller businesses routinely conduct international transactions. So it is more important than ever to know that the person at the other end of the phone may have different perceptions. It is vital to put in processes and training programs that help us communicate and welcome our differences with grace.

Communicating expectations

Compassionate communication creates followers and fosters relationships. Communicating compassionately involves setting and sharing clear expectations of the people we work with while showing genuine concern for their wellness. Compassionate communication becomes especially critical during organizational change and the launch of new projects.

Ramanathan Meyyappan, Senior Manager of IT Applications at VMWare, recollects the time he was charged with a technical upgrade of a mission-critical stack of software components whose stability and availability was important for VMWare's Customer Experience and his team's responsibility. Going by industry standards, it takes 18 months with the help of implementation partners. His team was set to deliver the project in 9 months entirely in-house.

Knowing the enormity of the task ahead for him and his colleagues, he took time off work to reflect on the best way to communicate with clarity and compassion. This is the letter he sent out to his Operations/Support team.

"**T**eam,

We have all spoken enough about how critical the XXX program is and the next 12-13 months in our career when we'll be heading on the journey together.

I feel, based on what we've done so far, that if we can't pull this off, then who else can.

At the same time, let's take a few minutes to remind ourselves the following:

1. We cannot be overconfident. That's too much of weight that pulls us down the drain and will increase our work pressure at critical junctures when we hit roadblocks.

2. Collaborate, using every single opportunity internally and externally, and remember - no question is a silly/stupid question to ask or address. Devote time to think, ask the right questions, and spend enough time with others. Also, try to play along even when silly/stupid questions are asked. We may end up finding out something that we had never thought about till then, which might emerge super-critical.

3. Plan your time properly and keep the team abreast of your plans as much as possible. Work-life balance and having

personal/family time when required is of utmost importance to ensure your mental balance during work.

4. Lightwave engagement we have with R&D is a supercritical one and is a potential VMworld success story next time around and, who knows, we may even get to present the same. We are fortunate with the kind of transparency and support we are receiving from the R&D team in this regard. If we hit roadblocks, the easiest option is to fall back to OID and make this work. But think of what kind of an opportunity we are set to lose if we give up. Considering this, I am sure, will bring the resolve and perseverance required to focus on resolving such roadblocks.

5. There can be situations where we might behave out of line or out of the ordinary with one another due to sheer pressure and frustration during the course. Remain calm and avoid conflicts during such situations, which is the last we want as a team. There is nothing personal.

6. If anyone of you thinks that any approach or decision or path we take is wrong, please convey it, and in the interest of the program and the team, everyone should listen to the same and make the course correction if the situation requires.

7. No individual is indispensable, and the team and the program are bigger than any individual. We have set our bars high, and hence, settling below our expectations isn't an available option for us.

8. Roadblocks are opportunities for us to learn to avoid/overcome future ones.

9. Take absolute care of your health, know your limits, and do not stretch beyond your limits. Short-term gains are not worth paying huge consequences in the future.

10. Be open to thinking out of the box to resolve issues creatively and efficiently.

These might sound too philosophical and motivational, but, based on my experiences and those I have been inspired by, these really work.

Let us sit tight, fasten our seatbelts, and look forward to what the challenging ride ahead has in store.**"**

Ramanathan's email clearly laid out the expectations and challenges, but also made sure the need for self-care was communicated. And he followed through with the spirit of the email.

The day of the scheduled delivery happened to be on Diwali, which is the biggest holiday in India. Despite this, every member of the Project team was willingly on-site, from 06:00 am to 10:30 pm, on a day that they would have spent celebrating with their families, because they were now united in purpose. This turned out to be one of the game-changing IT Deliverables (brewed in-house from scratch) for VMWare, saving the company enormous amounts of time and money, and in the process winning Ramanathan and his extended project team IT Risk-Taking award for the quarter from the office of the CIO of VMWare.

Tools for compassionate communication

One of my favorite tools for compassionate communication is **the five chairs exercise**. It involves (mentally) sitting on five chairs to gain the right perspectives for compassion in communication.

Let us imagine that you are a mid-level manager of a small team. One of the people you lead is Sara, who has been with your company for two years. She used to be a good employee, but for six months now she has been coming in late, leaving early, delaying her deliverables, and in general been a poor contributor. Last week she made an error in her report, which caused your supervisor to yell at you. You are justifiably angry with Sara.

Scenario 1: Sara walks into your room. You do not give her eye contact. You nod while looking at the computer. You have an arsenal of data on your computer screen to show how much she is at fault. You are frowning, your arms are crossed, and she can feel you are angry. In fact, you want her to know your disappointment. When you speak, your voice betrays your frustration. You look up and tell her very curtly, "I don't think you are a good match here. I have all your reports in front of me. I can see you have failed us repeatedly in the last six months. This is a company, not a charity. Either you shape up or quit. You have six more months before we re-evaluate you."

How will you feel at the end of the interaction? How will Sara feel? How better will your business outcomes be because of this conversation?

Now let us try a different approach. For this approach, we will take perspectives using the 5-chairs exercise.

1. Sitting on the chair of **Objective**, you ask, 'Why am I having this conversation? Is it to express my justified anger against Sara's performance? Or is it to find meaningful solutions to the situation and outline a path forward? It is to punish or heal?'

2. Sitting on the chair of **Perspective**, you ask, 'What if I were Sara? What should be happening to me that I would go from being a good performer to a poor one?'

3. Sitting on the chair of **Emotional Outcomes**, you ask, 'If I were Sara, how would I want this conversation to make me feel? Inspired to become my best self or wean and scared into performing?

4. Sitting on the chair of **The Kindest Option**, you remember that it is not just about Sara or you, but it is also about the team and the company. So you ask 'Of all the choices

for action laid out in front of me, what is the kindest option- one that would create win-win all around?'

5. Sitting on the final chair of **Clarity**, I ask, 'Now that I have gone through my internal dialogs, how can I communicate the message in a way that there is no ambiguity or confusion?'

Scenario 2: Sara walks into your room. You have all the data on your computer, but you are not worried about that. You usher Sara in with a smile, and ask her to sit down, ask how her day is. You then get into an honest conversation. Your palms are open, your body leans forward gently, and your kind intentions are evident in your eyes and voice.

"Sara," you say "You have been with us for two years and for the most part you have been a good employee. However, as you know, your work has been struggling in the past several months. I wanted to meet you to discuss this and understand how I can help you get past this phase."

Sara might say, "No, I am sorry, I will try harder," or she might become defensive (because she has been thinking about this meeting all night and she is trying to protect herself) and say, "No, everything is ok. You guys have been inconsiderate and piling up all kinds of work on me.'

But you are not drawn into the dialogs, because your objectives are clear. Therefore, you say, "I understand that the pace in our team is different now. However, I am worried that you are not showing up to your full potential here. You are capable of so much more. I am having this conversation to understand how we can really help you. I respect your privacy, but understanding your challenges can help us craft solutions together."

"I am sorry," Sara says, "I am going through a divorce. I am now handling my two kids, the divorce proceedings, and my work. My life is a mess" She is now tearing up.

You give her the due space and silence.

"Thank you for sharing a vulnerable moment. I am sorry to hear all that you are going through. As your colleagues, we would all like to help you navigate this difficult time. How about we figure out options, perhaps adjust your work times around your child drop off time, until this you tide over this situation? You could make up by contributing in other areas. How about you and I sit down and create a plan for your success here?'

How will Sara feel about the company at the end of this? Would she be more inspired to show up better at work? Would the human and business outcomes be better than Scenario 1?

Compassionate communication also involves knowing when to cut short an argument in our heads. In the heat of an argument, our executive centers are not firing. We need to have space and time to access our brain's executive centers. Often arguments can take tangents that have nothing to do with the original intent. This is where mindful pauses come in handy. Silence sometimes is the most compassionate communication.

Promoting compassionate communication

Compassionate communication works magic- vertically and laterally within organizations, and when organizations interface with their customers. As a leader in your organization, you have the capacity to direct the tone and flow of communication. Here are some ideas.

1. Model the compassionate communication you want to see in your team

2. Encourage mindful pauses before and during difficult conversations.

3. Create and communicate clear expectations of respect in all forms of communications- verbal or digital.

4. Be fair and fearless in addressing outliers to the cultural narrative of compassionate communication

5. Create physical reminders of compassionate communication throughout the workspace. For example, after teaching the five chairs exercise to your team, you could place images of the 5-chairs exercise, as reminders of the skill.

6. Recognize and reward those leaders in your organization who communicate compassionately while honoring business goals.

As an influencer in my organization, what processes can I set in place for people to communicate compassionately?

_____
_____
_____
_____
_____
_____
_____
_____
_____
_____
_____
_____
_____
_____
_____
_____
_____
_____

MY KEY TAKEAWAYS FROM THIS CHAPTER

_____
_____
_____
_____
_____
_____
_____
_____
_____
_____
_____
_____
_____
_____

Vulnerability

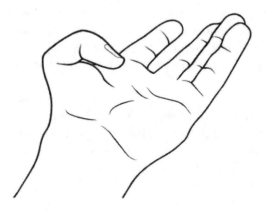

"And the day came when the risk to remain tight in a bud was more painful than the risk it took to blossom."
— Anais Nin

What is vulnerability?

Vulnerability is the courage to show up as our authentic selves, with our perfections and imperfections on display, simply because it is the right thing to do. Vulnerability encourages us to embrace the messiness of life fearlessly, and in doing so, creates compassionate responses. According to Vulnerability researcher **Dr. Brene Brown**, vulnerability is the greatest measure of courage.

Vulnerability is critical for growth. I think of vulnerability as the courage of a lobster to shed its shell. Lobsters are soft-bodied animals with hard shells. As their bodies grow, their shell remains rigid, making it uncomfortable for them to stay inside their shells. The discomfort triggers them to molt out of their shell and create a new one. A molted lobster looks like a black rubber toy, which then absorbs water and swells to its new size. At this time, until they can grow a new shell, lobsters are very vulnerable to prey. The process of growing a new shell takes a week or two. During this time, the lobsters go into hiding. When their shells are hard enough, they emerge strong, even regenerating lost claws in the process. Being vulnerable to the right people for the right reasons at the right time is critical for growth to happen. Vulnerability opens doors of opportunities because it opens our eyes to what we are missing.

Invulnerability is an illusion of strength. An invulnerable mind says that it cannot fail or appear weak. The illusion of invulnerability blocks growth. Imagine if a baby thinks, 'Everyone around me is walking. I cannot appear weak. I cannot let anyone know that I cannot walk, for if I try, I might fall, and that is weakness' So the baby, not having the courage to fall, decides not to try and spends all its life crawling. As ridiculous as that example sounds, that is true for us, the adults, on many levels. When we fail, and we will fail, our invulnerable brain manufactures excuses and untruths to hold on to the illusion of power.

Let me be vulnerable and share my own story.

Several years ago, I ran an in-home senior care agency. Before this, I had been a cancer drug discovery scientist. I had no experience seeing people's suffering. So this job, which I had chosen for myself, was a mismatch, from an emotional standpoint. Every time I visited my clients- most of them seniors with Alzheimer's or some major health issues- it affected me deeply. I would place myself in their emotional shoes, reinforcing my inner fear that there was a certain futility in living. I realize now that this was a fear that has deep roots in my psyche. Even though I was personalizing pain and practicing misguided empathy, which was increasingly depressing me, I did not acknowledge it to myself or anyone else. I come from a time and culture that said that real men don't cry. Men were supposed to be rock-like: no tears, no public display of emotions. Almost a year and a half after I started the senior care business, I lost my first client. I remember getting the call at 2 am that a gentleman whom my team had been caring for almost a year, had died. I could not sleep for the rest of the night. That morning, my wife found me sobbing in bed. That was a first, for her and me. It took me a lot of courage, overcoming a lifetime of conditioned beliefs, to open up to my wife that behind my rock-solid facade was an emotional mess. Only when I became vulnerable with her did I realize how much I had been sweeping under my emotional rug. With her encouragement, I visited a psychiatrist. I was diagnosed with severe depression. From there began a journey of healing. If I had not been courageous enough to open up to my wife, I would not have sought help. My cultural setting taught me that any mental health issue was hush-hush. My experiments with vulnerability taught me that I should be able to talk about my depression with the same guiltless openness as I would about my flu. My experiences with depression prompted me to understand empathy, to learn the difference between empathy and compassion, and through a series of events, become an evangelist and teacher of compassion.

How vulnerability shows up

There is something innately cathartic about being vulnerable. But catharsis or feeling better is not the intent or objective of vulnerability. Vulnerability shows up in many ways. But the common theme in all vulnerable experiences is courage. Here are some ways that vulnerability shows up in our lives.

- ➢ Vulnerability is acknowledging that I am lacking or suffering
- ➢ Vulnerability is seeking help when I am lacking or suffering
- ➢ Vulnerability is acknowledging mistakes
- ➢ Vulnerability is acknowledging fear
- ➢ Vulnerability if embracing uncertainty
- ➢ Vulnerability is stepping into action knowing that I can fail, knowing that action is my most authentic choice
- ➢ Vulnerability is sharing an unpopular opinion in a team meeting, just because it is the right thing to do
- ➢ Vulnerability is daring to take off my masks

> ➤ Vulnerability is taking ownership
> ➤ Vulnerability is giving honest feedback
> ➤ Vulnerability is daring to rekindle relationships after challenges
> ➤ Vulnerability is telling a difficult truth, even if the untruth is easier to tell
> ➤ Vulnerability is daring to acknowledge the best in a competitor
> ➤ Vulnerability is not hiding my limitations

Vulnerability blocks

We are afraid to be vulnerable for many reasons.

Fear of judgment and humiliation. No one wants to be the first to challenge an uncertainty and risk appearing the fool. This ties into a lack of psychological safety. If I am not fairly sure that expressing my opinion is not going to weaken my standing in the team, I would probably not venture to be the first to point out a problem, especially if it's not my challenge.

Previous negative experiences with lack of air cover. If I am vulnerable, and my leader uses the information I share to throw me under the bus, or simply watches others in my team take advantage of my vulnerability, my trust is breached. I would not risk exposing my mind to the team again.

Fear of being taken advantage of. Bob Vanourek, author of Triple Crown Leadership says, *"Trust is built when someone is vulnerable and not taken advantage of."* For some of us, it takes only one negative experience of someone taking advantage of us to drive us into our protective shell. Next time around, we will have a good reason not to be vulnerable.

Cultural uncertainty. Unless my team members and leaders model the level of vulnerability that is acceptable in my new company, I would rather not take the risk.

Misplaced expectations of self. 'I am super(wo)man; I can go it by myself, I am supposed to be the knowledge guru, I cannot fail' are some of the inner dialogues that block vulnerability.

Misunderstanding of vulnerability. Sometimes, the very discussion of being vulnerable scares us, because we misunderstand the intent of being vulnerable. Vulnerability does not have to be a sacrifice of privacy or power. Vulnerability is not a weakness. It is raw power.

Rewiring the brain for vulnerability

Rewiring the brain for vulnerability takes time and effort. Courage, Acceptance, and Wisdom are three behavioral constructs that help wire our brains for vulnerability.

1. Courage which manifests as action. Imagine a team leader who is about to admit to his management that his team has fallen short of the company's expectations by a large margin. His ego is hurting. The judgmental part of him is telling him that he is a failure as a leader. But he knows it must be done. So instead of passing the blame on 'untenable circumstances' and 'poor team performance', he stands up takes ownership of the shortcomings. He lays out the efforts that were done, acknowledges the errors in judgment, takes personal ownership of his failure as a leader, assures that the next quarter will be better, and outlines how this will be achieved. To practice this, he first needs to know himself- his values, why he does what he does, and what his leadership is about. Conviction comes from clarity. When a person is rooted in her truths, it is easy to be courageous.

People who know their strengths and weaknesses, who know and accept what makes them happy or unhappy, are the people who are most capable of being vulnerable. Knowing their own selves helps them stand firm in their vulnerable moments.

2. Acceptance of our flawed humanity and situational outcomes.

Accepting our flawed humanity

In having vulnerable conversations, it helps to remember one of the constructs of self-compassion- that we are all one shared humanity. It is okay to fail. It is okay to be vulnerable about our failures. When we accept that we are not the only ones to fail, it is easy for us to be vulnerable. If anyone comes across as infallible, they are likely very good at pretend play. If we fail and are courageous about expressing it boldly, we are in a better off place than someone who has failed but does not dare to be open about it.

And our failures may not be as big as they might seem in the moment. I remember reading a story about a famous baseball player who lost the match for his team by fumbling his last ball. A reporter asked him about how, in spite of his great loss, he seemed cheerful. This is what he said: *"There are a billion people in China who will wake up tomorrow morning and not care that I won or lost. So, relax!"*

It helps to know that our failures may also inspire others. As flawed human beings, we always look up to the failures, and subsequent successes, of our idols. Here is one of the vulnerability statements I look up to for inspiration when I am down. This is from **Michael Jordan**, one of Basketballs' enduring superstars.

"I've missed more than 9000 shots in my career. I've lost almost 300 games. 26 times, I've been trusted to take the game winning shot and missed. I've failed over and over and over again in my life. And that is why I succeed."

Accepting outcomes

It becomes easier to be vulnerable when we are not tied to specific outcomes of our vulnerability. Sometimes it is better not to overthink the ramifications of a vulnerable act. We are vulnerable because it is the right thing to do, no more, no less . How the people we have chosen to be vulnerable with are going to interpret and process our vulnerability is not entirely under our control. So when the decision has been made, and the people I want to be vulnerable with are chosen, it is better to let loose and be open to the outcomes. Whatever happens, will be either a gift or a lesson, and through them, we will grow.

3. Wisdom is knowing who deserves my trust

As Dr.Brene Brown points out

'If we share our shame story with the wrong person, they can easily become one more piece of flying debris in an already dangerous storm.'

To be wise about our choices of who we are vulnerable to is what will help us continue to be vulnerable. I use the W4 questions to understand who deserves my trust.

Why?   **Who?**

Where?   **When?**

These four questions help me understand if I am ready to open up to someone or not. Unfortunately, trust is built in small increments, in iterative efforts of trial and error. Sometimes we trust with our best judgment, and the trust is broken. This is where we make a choice- to retreat into our shells or push forward with courage toward growth.

These are similar to the questions that help me understand if I will become a doormat giver or not (see the chapter on Abundance

Mindset). Ultimately, being vulnerable should be a comfortable balance between self-compassion and compassion.

Shelley Winner, Surface Specialist at Microsoft Corporation, shares this powerful experience with vulnerability.

"I made some unfortunate choices when I was young. I dabbled in drugs very early and eventually started dealing them. Eventually, I was caught by the police in a sting operation. I was sentenced to time in prison. My son was born during my period of incarceration. I knew I had to turn my life around, at least for the sake of my son. I worked extremely hard while at prison, studying and getting myself qualified for jobs in the world outside. When I was released from prison, I faced the difficult task of landing a job. The stigma associated with my past made it difficult for me to find a meaningful position. Through perseverance and effort, and the support of some very kind mentors, I finally landed a position with a global software company. This was not just a job for me. I knew this was my one big opportunity to redeem myself. I gave my job the very best of my commitment and effort, with the result that within the first months of my joining the company, I was recognized as a most valuable player.

The praise and recognition that I received for my efforts naturally generated envy in some of my colleagues. Two of my colleagues were particularly unhappy about the attention my work was generating. I had always been open about my past, so this was an easy point for them to judge me and undermine me. Every small error and every little lapse on my part was being unduly escalated, to the point that even my leadership was getting annoyed. I was upset because I knew my colleagues were being unkind and unfair to me, and judging me for a past that I was actively trying to step away from. It became difficult for me to be happy and productive at work with all the negativity around. So, after due thought, I decided on the most courageous course of action I could think of- I decided to be vulnerable. I reached out to these two colleagues individually and asked them out for coffee. They were surprised, but they did accept. In these one-on-one conversations, I was brutally honest. I shared my story, I told them about the struggles that I was facing as an ex-convict trying to set up a new life, I shared my understanding about how their actions were hurting me, and how much it would mean for me to be able to work without judgments or unfairness in my workplace. My colleagues were surprised by my honesty, but my vulnerability worked. That was the end of the bullying. I would not say that these two people became my best friends, but we became great colleagues, and all that because I chose vulnerability in the face of bullying."**

Experiments with vulnerability
Exercise 1: Who are three people I am vulnerable with? Why am I vulnerable to them? Are there any common themes that show up?
Does this tell me who I feel deserve my trust?

_____

_____

_____

_____

_____

_____

_____

_____

_____

_____

_____

_____

_____

_____

_____

_____

Exercise 2: At this time in my life, who are the people I need to be vulnerable to? How will I know if they are ready for my trust (W4: Why, Who, When, Where)?

_____

_____

_____

_____

_____

_____

_____

_____

_____

_____

_____

_____

_____

_____

_____

_____

_____

_____

_____

Vulnerability and Compassion

Being vulnerable is an act of self-compassion. Being vulnerable allows us to accept things as they are, and let go of failings. Vulnerability is recognizing that this moment is not the end of the game. To be free of the chains of perception that invulnerability has created is liberating.

Vulnerability fights shame. As researchers point out, guilt and shame are two different things. Guilt is the realization that we have done something wrong. Shame is the feeling that we are wrong. Guilt is tied to an act. Shame is tied to our self-worth. Vulnerability allows us to get the clarity that we are not the mistakes we make, and whatever our mistakes, we are still worthy.

Vulnerability prompts reciprocity. Our vulnerability gives people the permission to be vulnerable themselves. It opens the doors for trust to be created. Research confirms a positive relationship between employee trust and workplace performance. A 2002 study[19] by Watson Wyatt shows that high-trust companies outperformed low-trust companies in total return to shareholders by 286%. A 2013 survey of business professionals concurs: teams with high trust outperform teams that don't trust each other[20]. A distrustful culture leads to inefficiency and costly turnovers. Vulnerability in the workplace creates trust and connection. Even from a purely business consideration, it pays to be vulnerable.

Just as we need skills to be vulnerable, we also need the skills to *receive vulnerability*. A powerful act of compassion is to embrace a person's vulnerable moment without judgment and seek to help the person on their journey. It takes small acts of consciously letting go of ego, preconceived notions, fears, and assumptions to receive vulnerability and create trust.

One of the acts of vulnerability as a leader is the capacity to take ownership of situations that go wrong. When one of the top advisers of his 2016 presidential campaign was accused of forcibly kissing a young female staffer, Bernie Sanders made a public apology: "To the women in our campaign who were harassed or mistreated, I apologize," he added. "Our standards, our procedures, our safeguards, were clearly inadequate." Many leaders tout that the buck stops with them, but not many have the courage to put that into action in times of challenge.

Remembering to be curious about the roots of our conditioning and becoming rooted in our sense of purpose helps practice and receive vulnerability. As Dr. Brene Brown says, *"Owning our story can be hard but not nearly as difficult as spending our lives running from it. Embracing our vulnerabilities is risky but not nearly as dangerous as giving up on love, belonging, and joy—the experiences that make us the most vulnerable. Only when we are brave enough to explore the darkness will we discover the infinite power of our light."*

Here is a simple team exercise to try to help people become aware of their resistance to vulnerability:

This is an exercise you can try in your team meeting. **Have your team members pair up and sit facing each other. For two minutes, teammates look into each other's eyes (but not stare). At the end of the exercise, they share with the group how they felt looking into their partner's eyes (discomfort, mind wandering, anxiety, etc.).** I suspect that this will be far more challenging for people than it sounds on paper. I did this exercise at a bank, and two male colleagues happened to be paired with each other. In the end, one of them said that this was the most uncomfortable experience he had had and that he realized that he had not even taken the time to look into his wife's eyes intentionally without judgment!

This is a question to be discussed as a team in your workplace.

What will you need to be vulnerable about as a team or organization? How will you allow vulnerability to manifest in your workplace?

_____

_____

_____

_____

_____

_____

_____

_____

_____

_____

_____

_____

_____

_____

_____

_____

MY KEY TAKEAWAYS FROM THIS CHAPTER

_____

_____

_____

_____

_____

_____

_____

_____

_____

_____

_____

_____

_____

_____

_____

Big-picture thinking

"The Bushmen in the Kalahari Desert talk about the 'two hungers'. There is the Great Hunger and there is the Little Hunger. The Little Hunger wants food for the belly; but the Great Hunger, the greatest hunger of all, is the hunger for meaning..."- **Laurens van der Post**

What is big-picture thinking?

Big-picture thinking is the ability to experience life with perspective and purpose. With big-picture mindset, we are able to take the ten-thousand-foot view of the situation and see challenges for what they are, without getting stuck in the details. With big-picture thinking, we are able to handle difficult triggers with grace and make compassionate decisions. When we train our minds to soar above the messiness of current challenges, we can practice responses that create win-win solutions.

Big-picture thinking is interwoven into the wisdom of the other pillars of compassion. Big-picture thinking allows us to act proactively rather than reactively. As we think and practice the big-picture mindset, we are able to become abundant. We are able to put people first and embrace the shared oneness of our humanity. We are able to become vulnerable. This helps avoid unnecessary conflict at work and creates emotional resilience. Cultivated as a leadership habit, big-picture thinking can help manage people and time with grace, and help turn challenges into opportunities.

Let us say I am a team manager giving a presentation to my team on the updated company goals for the next two quarters. I could spend countless hours over creating a perfect slide deck for a presentation. I could spend days locked in dialog with a colleague about why blue, not pink, is a better background color for the slides, or why a particular font is better than another. Big-picture thinking allows me to shake myself away from the details-trap and ask, how much this presentation is going to impact my real goals-which is to get my team members on board with the changes effectively? Then I realize that the presentation is only to kick-start the change and that a lot more time and energy is needed for the follow-up steps. This will consequently allow me to refocus my time on work that can create the most impact.

In 1896 Italian economist Vilfredo Pareto demonstrated that 80% of land in Italy was owned by 20% of the population. Later on, the 80-20 distribution was found to hold true for many other situations. Management consultant Joseph Juran summarized it as the **Pareto principle**, which states that roughly 80% of effects arise from 20% of causes. For example, 20% of our efforts at work may lead us to 80% of the success in our professional journeys. Big-picture thinking allows us to focus on the 20% that matters.

Big-picture thinking has two essential facets. One is the ability to think in perspective. The other is to be rooted to purpose.

Perspective thinking

Perspective thinking allows us to see challenges in context and realize that we are bigger than our circumstances.

To think in perspective is to be able to contrast and reframe our current challenge against a bigger universal reality. We value experiences by contrasting them to expectations created by our environment and past experiences. Perspective thinking may seem like a philosophical exercise at first, but the value of understanding the yardstick against which we ultimately measure our personal realities cannot be underestimated.

Perspective thinking not only can help reframe our personal challenges; it also helps reframe the challenges of those we lead. It helps provide latitude for the mistakes of others, extend understanding to those who are struggling, and make meaningful decisions while dealing with them.

When I face challenging situations, I lean into my library of perspective questions. These questions help reframe my thinking.

"How big is my problem, really?"

"How big will this challenge seem to be three years from now?"

"If this is an opportunity disguised as a problem, how should I be looking at it differently?"

"How much of my challenge is reality, and how much is made up by fear?"

"What really are my actionable choices, and what is blocking me from making them?"

REFRAMING PERSPECTIVES

Here is a little thought exercise in perspective thinking

Our universe formed 13.5 billion years ago. Earth formed 4.5 billion years ago. A billion years later, the first life started appearing on the planet in the form of cyanobacteria. The first vertebrates appeared in the oceans about 530 million years ago. About 490 million years ago, the first green plants appeared on land. Less than 100 million years later, the first amphibians ventured onto land. From the amphibians rose the reptiles, the birds and the mammals.

At a very recent 3.9 million years ago, the first hominid creatures formed. Less than 2 million years later, these hominids had evolved to create stone tools. The first use of fire happened 790,000 years ago. A meager 11,400 years ago, humans developed agriculture and began domesticating livestock. The pyramids of Giza were built 4500 years ago. As we discussed at the beginning of the book, the first industrial revolution started in the late 18th century with the discovery of steam power, mechanical production, and railroads. A hundred years later, the second industrial revolution involving assembly lines, electrical power, and mass production began. In the late 1900s, humanity entered the third industrial revolution with automated production, electronics, and computers. Now in the early 2000s, we are already in our fourth industrial revolution with Artificial Intelligence, big data, and robotics driving our lives. The molecules that make us, the air that we breathe in, the food that we eat- are the same ones that make the stars. We are recycled products. We were dinosaurs once, and we will be our progeny ten thousand years from now. 'I' is simply a consciousness passing through a physical plane. And our earth is one of 30 billion planets in our galaxy alone, and there are 100 billion galaxies in our observable universe. And we still do not know how many universes there are out there. And all of these considerations prompt us to ask:

'How significant am I?'

But look inward into our own bodies, and we realize that there is enough complexity as there is in the universe itself. Each of us humans is made of 37 trillion cells, each cell having close to 2 trillion molecules working in perfect harmony. And these cells are forever busy, communicating with their neighbors, sending signals inward, consuming and creating energy, multiplying and dying in a perfect dance, so that each of us can uniquely experience this magic called life. Are we mere accidents? I believe not. I believe, as temporal as we are, we are all part of a perfect semi-autonomous design.

And all these considerations prompt us to wonder:

'How significant I am!"

As we place our biggest problems in the altar of these considerations, the worst of fears cave in. There is an interesting perspective I read in' Tuesdays with Morrie' by **Mitch Albom**. It goes like this, *"Every day, have a little bird on your shoulder that asks, 'Is today the day? Am I ready? Am I doing all I need to do? Am I being the person I want to be? Is today the day I die?"*

Reminders of the possibility of our own demise is a powerful perspective tool. It fosters gratitude and surprisingly, happiness. Thinking of our own mortality allows us to make compassionate decisions that we otherwise may not. In Bhutan, one of the happiest countries in the world, everyone is expected to contemplate death five times every day!

What if you had a little bird on your shoulder reminding you that today could be the last day on this planet? How different would your interactions be?

I find that taking time to reflect and compare my problems against my bigger vision of life and leadership helps me make meaningful choices. Perspective thinking creates more compassion, grace, and clarity. When our employees fail, for example, instead of reacting with disappointment or anger, what if we consciously step back to ask:

- "What does this failure mean in the bigger picture of the organization?"
- "What does it mean in the context of this employee's life cycle with the company?"
- "What can I do that can enable this person's growth, while still meeting work objectives?"
- "In the 10,000-feet view of things, how devastating is this mistake?"

Here are some exercises you can do to help you build the perspective thinking habit.

Create your personal 'treasure-box' of perspective questions. This is your personal collection of all the questions that can help you look at challenges you encounter in a different light.

Think of a challenge from your past that seemed insurmountable at that time, but which you have now overcome. Reflect on how the biggest challenges in your life have found closure with time. What does that mean for your current challenge?

_____
_____
_____
_____
_____
_____
_____
_____
_____
_____
_____
_____
_____
_____
_____
_____
_____

STRATEGY

Strategy goes hand in glove with perspective thinking. _Strategy is being able to visualize the outcome and knowing how to get there._ In the context of leadership, this means knowing what you want to achieve with your leadership role and having a roadmap to reach your target.

Remember that your leadership goal is not a job function or title. Rather, it is defining what impact you will leave on the world because of your leadership, and how you would have influenced others positively as a result. Defining your leadership legacy is the first step. Creating a broad vision of how you will make that happen is your second step.

Let me challenge you to come up with your personal leadership strategy statement. But limit your strategy statement to less than 50 words.

A sample could read something like this:

"I will be a high impact leader, helping all the people I lead achieve career and personal excellence, by continually applying myself to personal growth, education and persistent action."

There are no perfect strategy statements. Go with whatever is authentic and meaningful for you at this time in your life. Keep your strategy statement in a place where you can see it often. Use it as a yardstick when you think in perspective.

_____

_____

_____

_____

_____

_____

Purpose

Purpose is the 'Why' of our existence. A great way to think of purpose is the Okinawan philosophy of **'Ikigai'**. 'Ikigai' roughly translates to 'a reason for being'. Everyone needs to know their reason for being- why we do what we do, what motivates us, what wakes us up wanting to give our best to the world with love, what makes us happy, what enriches our world and our relationships, what we want to leave behind as our legacy. Without purpose, we are rudderless ships in the ocean. We go everywhere, but we go nowhere.

There are many life-purpose exercises. Here is one I created for my coachees.

THE LIFE PURPOSE CANVAS

The objective of the Life Purpose Canvas is to help you gain more clarity on the 'why' of your life journeys, and help you create an action plan for a life of meaning and action.

Please take your time working on this. You can potentially influence a lifetime of experiences with this experience. You can either write on these pages or use sticky notes to write down the answers, whichever is convenient for you.

There are three steps to this process. Step 1 and 2 are meant to be reflections and can set the context for the Life purpose canvas, which is Step 3.

Step 1: This is where you were.

Every experience in our life, whether by deliberate choice or seemingly accidental, tells us something about our subconscious constructs. If we care to stop and look back without fear, we could end up with valuable personal insights.

Please write down what is authentic for you. Do not overthink. Let your emotions talk.

Use this to complete A, B and C on the next slide.

Step-1: Understanding my roots

Why did I choose my educational/career path?	Why do I wish I had done instead?
What was my proudest moment?	**My Journeys**
	How did I choose relationships I am most proud of?
What are my non-negotiable values?	
	What is it about people I admire most?

Step 1: Study your responses. What are some common themes?

A._____

B._____

C._____

Step 2: This is where you want to be.

This legacy exercise, where you imagine your own death and think of all the things that you would want people to remember you by, is difficult but extremely powerful. Clarity on your legacy can set the context for your current plan of action.

Please write down what is authentic for you. Do not overthink. Let your emotions talk.

Use this to complete D, E, F in the next image.

Step-2: Defining my legacy

How would I like to be described in my eulogy?	Why are these descriptions important for me?

My Desired Footprint

Step 2: Top adjectives I would like to hear in my eulogy

D. _____

E. _____

F. _____

Step 3: Life purpose canvas.

Steps 1 and 2 have set the intellectual and emotional context for creating your life purpose canvas. Fill in boxes 1 through 5 first. Look for common themes. Use these responses to complete boxes 6 through 9.

Step-3: Life purpose canvas.

Fill in boxes 1 through 5 first. Use these responses to complete boxes 6 through 9

1	2	3	4	5
Doing these spark joy in me (passion)	Doing these makes me feel peaceful	When I do these I feel authentic.	When I do these I feel connected to a higher power	Doing these energizes me

My Life Purpose

6	7	8	9
Of the list from boxes 1 through 5, these will stretch me to grow	What careers/financial opportunities will align to my values from boxes 1 through 5?	Of the list from 1 through 5, I can do these to improve the world and its residents	Of the list from boxes 1 through 5, these bring me closer to my legacy.

You are almost done!

Move on to the next image to draft your life purpose statement. Use answers from your sheets above to fill in the spaces.

Modify until it feels just right for you.

My life purpose statement

I am a self aware, purpose driven individual on a path of positively impacting on my world.

I am unique in my strengths and my skills.

In my past being/doing (A) ------------ (B)------------ and (C)------------ have helped me shine.

As I move forward, I commit to a life of abundance in my career as ------------ (box 7).

I commit to improving my world by ------------ (box 8).

I commit to thriving, because being/doing ------------,

-- (input from boxes 1 through 6) bring me joy, energize me, bring me peace, and help me grow beyond the limits I currently see.

By living a purpose aligned life, when my journey is done, the world will remember me as (D)------------,

(E)------------ and (F)------------.

That's it!

Try and think about how you can influence your actions with your new-found clarity. Your future is for you to mold!

An additional note:

Please try to keep this completed work for future reference. Your current life purpose statement is a living, breathing document of your current realities. As you change, so will your 'why's' and 'how's'. Do plan to revisit this whenever you need clarity in your life.

You are the artist painting your life canvas!

As you approach challenges rooted in purpose and perspective, it is easy to become proactively compassionate in response to situations. We are able to reframe situations in ways that allow for responses that alleviate suffering.

Applying big-picture thinking at work

Big-picture thinking can be a powerful tool for navigating life and leadership challenges. It can create resilience and prevent conflict. Thinking in perspective and having a clearly defined strategy will help in big-picture thinking. Making a habit of big-picture thinking can help you be a compassionate leader and create more engaged employees and stronger business outcomes.

What opportunities do you see for applying big picture thinking in your workplace?

_____

_____

_____

_____

_____

_____

_____

_____

_____

_____

_____

_____

_____

_____

MY KEY TAKEAWAYS FROM THIS CHAPTER

_____

_____

_____

_____

_____

_____

_____

_____

_____

_____

_____

_____

_____

_____

_____

_____

Gratitude

"Gratitude is the ability to experience life as a gift. It liberates us from the prison of self-preoccupation."
— **John Ortberg**

What is Gratitude?

Gratitude is the skill to step away from inner dialogs of entitlement and comparison, and acknowledge that everything we are and have is a blessing.

Gratitude is a feeling- not an intellectual exercise. Sometimes we realize the value of what we have only when we lose it. People we take for granted and complain about become valuable when they leave. Those slightly crooked eyes that we are ashamed of becomes so precious when we are about to lose it to disease. The colleague who annoys us with his football stories at work, seems like a blessing in retrospect, when he is replaced by a conniving manipulator. We often do not see people, relationships, and assets as blessings because we are caught in the illusion of permanence.

Narayan Krishan, the **Founder of Akshaya Trust, India** and one of the top 10 **CNN hero nominees of 2010**, shared this nugget with me.

'When you are giving alms, your palms are facing downward. How much time will it take for your palms that are face down to turn and face the sky and become the receiver of alms? It takes very little for the giver to become the receiver.'

Krishnan knows. He has been part of countless human stories- rescuing mentally ill, destitute people in his hometown of Madurai and rehabilitating them with grace and dignity. Krishnan has done this with a zealousness that is almost superhuman. Leaving behind a promising career as a five-star chef when he saw a mentally ill man eating his fecal waste, Krishnan has spent almost two decades being compassion. One of the big takeaways from his journeys:' Do not take anything or anyone for granted. Every moment is an opportunity for gratitude' You can learn more about Narayanan Krishnan and his work at http://www.akshayatrust.org.

Why gratitude?

'Gratitude can transform common days into thanksgivings, turn routine jobs into joy, and change ordinary opportunities into blessings' — **William Arthur Ward**

The impact of feeling and expressing gratitude on personal and professional life cannot be overemphasized. Feeling gratitude creates contentment, balance, and humility. Feeling gratitude helps us appreciate the value of others. Feeling grateful for others prompts authentic external expressions of gratitude. Master salesman and author, Zig Ziglar said that *'Gratitude is the healthiest of all human emotions. The more you express gratitude for what you have, the more likely you will have even more to express gratitude for.'*

Expressions of gratitude socially evolved to demonstrate fairness and reciprocity. When members of a social group fail to acknowledge and reciprocate, they become social outcasts. Researchers show that the expression of gratitude may serve to communicate reciprocal engagement and to prevent being seen as a "free-loader," which could end in social punishment[21].

Expressions of gratitude strengthen relationships and brings people together. And these can be simple habits. For example, in our home, we have a nighttime gratitude habit that involves each member of our family sharing three things that we are thankful for the day past. It helps us to bond, and see that in spite of all the challenges the days bring, we go to bed feeling happier knowing that we have something to be thankful for.

Below is a little story someone shared with me about the power of gratitude.

A man came to a psychiatrist seeking help for his failing marriage.

"She is not the woman I married fifteen years ago," he complained. "She is hard-headed, argumentative and judgmental. I have no peace when she is with me. I should divorce her".

The psychiatrist gave the man a good hearing and agreed that divorce was the best option if things did not improve.

"But I want you to try out something," he told the man. "Starting today, I want you to pay attention to all the good things your wife is doing. And make sure you appreciate her for that. Be effusive in your praise, and try to be less biased and critical. And always be sincere in your appreciation. Do this consistently for a month. Then come back, and we will discuss the divorce".

The man agreed.

That evening, when his wife made dinner, he savored it as he had in the early days of their courtship. After dinner, he thanked her sincerely for her cooking. His wife looked at him with suspicion but kept quiet. The next morning he found opportunities to thank her for breakfast, for his laundered clothes and their clean house.

"What is your game?" she asked him, "What do you want from me?"

"Nothing," he replied. "I just think I haven't been appreciative enough for all the good things you do at home."

She smirked at him and walked away, but there was a spring in her step as she did the usual chores around the house, and dinner that night had an extra touch of elegance. Through the day before he continued to express his gratitude for her efforts.

Two days in, she could see that he was really trying. And unconsciously, she too began to notice and appreciate the ways he was contributing to the family.

Thirty days later, the psychiatrist called the man to check on him.

"Have you decided on your divorce?" asked the psychiatrist.

"Divorce? No way" replied the man. "I never realized how much she means to me until I started noticing and being thankful for her gifts. And my gratitude allowed her to do the same for me. We have never been happier or more in love".

Multiple studies show that gratitude is good for the body. People who feel gratitude have fewer aches and pains, have reduced blood pressure and show increased self-care. Research also demonstrates that gratitude reduces negativity and reduces depression. Gratitude also improves resilience and reduces post-traumatic stress disorders.

Gratitude is a success magnet. There are many stories that illustrate that gratitude rewires not just us, but also the universe we live in and creates abundance.

Take the case of John Kralik. John was a lawyer who was in a very bad situation. At 53, he was losing everything of value in his life- a painful second divorce, children who were growing distant, a failing law firm and dying professional dreams. Walking on the hills near Los Angeles, John made a life-changing decision. He decided to think of and thank people in his life. He set himself an ambitious goal- one handwritten thank you note a day for 365 days. So, day after day, he wrote thank-you notes for the kindnesses he had received in his life- to family, friends, and acquaintances. He wrote those notes without expectations of help for his challenges, but in doing so, he had triggered a universal law- the law of reciprocity. Slowly people began to reach out to him- people who truly cared about him and wanted his success. His 365 thank you notes brought him back financial gain, friendships, physical health, and inner peace. He documents his journey in a beautiful memoir called '365 Thank Yous'.

In an article published in Psychotherapy Research in 2015, researchers showed that gratitude writing had significantly improved mental health compared to those who wrote about profound life experiences or only underwent counseling. Research by Glen Fox and Colleagues at the University of Southern California shows that when subjects were exposed to gratitude stories and asked to rate the gratitude they felt, the gratitude ratings correlated with brain activity in the anterior cingulate cortex and medial prefrontal cortex[22]. This is one of the parts of the brain, which we discussed as being activated during compassion practices. Activity of this brain region has been related to socially driven interactions and empathy-driven responses[23].

Our gratitude impacts people in ways we may not foresee. **Dani Saveker, Founder, Glas.life** and **Inspire Kindness** has done more than a thousand daily acts of kindness- one act of kindness a day. She started this out as a month-long experiment of performing one kind act per day. Being kind, a value she deeply believed in, was her way of healing from traumatic life experiences.

"I found that kindness is the antidote to judgment," she shares. "I decided to follow the definition of kindness that asks to give without exception or expectation. Remove the expectation, don't wait for a thank you, and do not decide who has a right to receive my kindness. I left notes and books in coffee shops, baked cakes, bought stuff for homeless people. About 21 days into the experiment, after doing an act of kindness, I caught myself reacting poorly to a triggered situation. It was a wake-up moment. I realized my doing an act of kindness earlier that day did not give me permission to behave poorly in a different situation. I realized then that kindness was not about 'doing' but about 'being'. I had initially planned this kindness experiment to continue for a month. I realized on that day I had a lot more to learn. So one month of kindness acts became two, and soon three years had passed. I realized the power of human connection that comes with kindness, and the ripple effects that spread out. Imagine buying an extra item while shopping and asking the person in the checkout counter to pass it on to someone else in line. A simple act like this ripples out- the person who is receiving the item is moved, the girl at the checkout counter is moved because she now has great news for someone, others in the queue are watching and being inspired. Kindness requires courage, hard work, thought, effort, not taking the easy option of judgment, but to really become conscious of the decisions and choices we make, and to sometimes be the person to stand up and say I won't accept this behavior. Whatever is happening to you, there is always an opportunity to practice kindness. I did this without expectation, but the kindness came back to me a hundredfold. On the one-hundredth day of doing my daily acts of kindness, I decided to make the day memorable by sending out thank you notes to people in my life. I shared that I was doing my everyday acts of kindness and that I was taking the opportunity to thank one-hundred people in my life, and that they were one of my one-hundred. I then added personalized short notes for each person I was reaching out to (it took me six hours), telling them one thing I really admired about them. Everything from, "I love how you managed to come through that difficult time' to 'I love how you are a tiger mom when it comes to protecting your children' to 'I love how you helped me out'. About after the eighth message was out, I started hearing back from people. 'Do you know how much I needed to hear that' "Thank you for reaching out. I have been in a dark place, and your words meant so much to me' The universe was using me to heal people through my expressions of gratitude. **"**

Deepak Chopra, teacher and author, says *'Gratitude is the open door to the power, the wisdom, the creativity of the universe. You open the door through gratitude'* Sometimes we keep this door closed because of a sense of entitlement, fear, limiting beliefs, and short-sightedness.

One of the big blocks to gratitude is comparison. Our brain processes everything it encounters relative to something else. If that something else is bigger and better than us, then we are lacking and it makes us unhappy, and therefore less prone to gratitude. If what we compare is less than us, we feel pride and sometimes drawn into ego. A better framework of comparison is based on needs rather than comparison. It helps to pause before 'I deserve' thinking and ask 'Why do I deserve?'. This is a powerful tool to step away from entitlement and ground ourselves into gratitude.

What challenges do I face in feeling and expressing gratitude? What can I do about them?

_____

_____

_____

_____

_____

_____

_____

_____

_____

_____

_____

_____

_____

_____

_____

Gratitude as a compassion pillar

Gratitude is probably the most emotionally gratifying of the 9 pillars of compassion. The brain can be rewired for gratitude. Again like all other compassion pillars it takes time and effort. An enemy of gratitude is entitlement. One of the ways to feel gratitude is to imagine losing the things we feel entitled about. I wake up on the wrong side of the bed- but what if I did not have a bed to wake up from? I have a cluttered house that drives me crazy- but what if I did not have a house?

Remembering that anything we have without the contribution of a thousand hands, seen and unseen, helps receive our gifts with due gratefulness. Here is a little exercise to try out.

I call this the **Icnhhw** exercise. Take one aspect or achievement in your life you are currently feeling blessed about. Say, a successful career, a great relationship, financial success.

Using the phrase, **'it could not have happened without** (icnhhw)...',

As an example:

I am feeling so blessed to be in a job that makes me so happy, and helps make a difference in the world. Icnhhw the support of my incredible wife who believed in my unconventional journey. Icnhhw the guidance of my amazing mentors who gave generously of their time and wisdom. Icnhhw friends who brought my training into their workplaces. Icnhhw the amazing people who attended my programs and validated my training. Icnhhw my collaborators who added value every step of my effort.

What is your Icnhhw experience?

_____

_____

_____

_____

_____

_____

_____

_____

_____

_____

_____

_____

_____

_____

_____

Gratitude evokes reciprocity. Here is why. We live in an age of information overload. There are so many things, electronic and otherwise, vying for our mental real estate at any given time. Only the most dramatic, only the most scandalous things even make it to our brains. Still, whatever the information overload, whenever I read or hear something about me, my ears perk up, my heart races, my brain focuses- because now I have managed to occupy the mental real estate of another individual. This is the power of recognition. If what I read or see about myself is kind, I lower my defenses. Suddenly this person who was kind to me is, in turn, occupying some of my mental real estate. In my lowered state of resistance, I consider the person who was kind to me in a kind light. I remember that I have good things to say and share about this person. If I don't respond or share a kind thing about the other person, it becomes unfinished business. The bias of the Zeigarnik effect, which does not allow for unfinished business to occupy the brain, kicks in. I reciprocate the kindness. While this interpretation of reciprocity may sound transactional, it is a reflection of reality.

To practice gratitude, it helps to think perspective. Consider this perspective from **Dr. James Doty**

"So often we complain about our situations. But if one reflects, 50% of the world lives on 2$ or less. If we keep that in mind, we realize we have very little to complain about. Most of us in the west have food, security, shelter. Unfortunately though, and this is a plague of western society and wealthy people, instead of being satisfied with what you have, we look at others who have more and become jealous. We want to be like them, and it upsets us. When in fact, we should be looking the other direction and saying, 'Wow, I am so blessed. I am so thankful. There are so many people who have much less than I, how can I possibly complain?'

It is not the event that creates happiness, but it is how you respond to the event that creates happiness. As an example, at one point, I was a very successful entrepreneur, and in a matter of six weeks, I lost close to 80 million dollars and became effectively bankrupt. I had to sell a lot of things. Someone said to me, 'Oh my

God, how can you even wake up in the morning? Your life is ruined!'

I laughed. I said, 'I am healthy. I am a neurosurgeon. In my job as a neurosurgeon, I am paid better than 99.9% of the population in the United States. How can I possibly complain about anything? I am blessed.**"**

You can read more about Dr. Doty's incredible journey in his international best-seller, 'Into the Magic Shop'.

Rajesh Setty, author, speaker, and serial entrepreneur is a visionary evangelist of gratitude and creator of *Thoughtful Cards*, which personalizes opportunities for expressing gratitude in workplaces. Rajesh proposes that one of the ways to grateful living is to re-label all life events as either Gifts or as Lessons. As simple as this exercise is, it can be surprisingly challenging and transforming!

All of us are where we are because of the giants whose shoulders carried us. Our memories are frail, so we need to create habits to remember. Not everything in life is transactional. We give just because, and thank just because. No one likes a person who takes advantage. Thank people when they have no longer have anything to give to you.

Receiving gratitude

It is just as important to be open to receiving gratitude as it is to give gratitude. There are some cultural elements that can come in the way of receiving gratitude. In the microculture that I grew up in, it was considered polite to not accept gratitude. So if someone thanked me, my knee jerk response was to deflect it back to them or to someone else. I did this until someone pointed out to me that a thank you was a gift, and I was being rude, not polite, by refusing it.

It takes a certain mindset of vulnerability to accept gratitude. Accepting the gratitude of others is not a weakness. We may be empowering someone by receiving their gratitude. This, like all limiting beliefs, needs to be faced head-on.

Some of us are primed to viewing gratitude with suspicion and skepticism. This often stems from bitter past experiences. For example, I might think: 'The person is thanking me because he/she is expecting something from me.' If this thought come up for me, I tell myself that may be true, but handling expectations is a different decision for a different moment in time.

Scarcity thinking also plays into the gratitude space as well. It is the idea that if someone thanks me for something nice I did, and if I accepted the thanks the score will be settled, and that would not be ok because what I did deserves more than a perfunctory thanks, and I want that person to feel indebted to me at some level. This is the matcher's mindset toward gratitude. My most compassionate argument to this is, if there is so much baggage around your giving in this case, perhaps it is better not to give at all?

Gratitude in the workplace

Authentic expressions of gratitude for colleagues, through word and action, helps them feel valued as individuals and inspire them to show up as better versions of themselves.

Expressions of gratitude do not have to be grand gestures. They can be simple, spontaneous everyday acts. Here are some gratitude exercises that you can experiment within your workplace.

Email your immediate circle of colleagues with gratitude.

Let's say there are 16 people in your team. Everyone sends out 15 personalized one-liner emails, thanking each person for one unique way they've added value to the workplace. You will, in turn, receive 15 emails- one from each of your colleagues. Simple, effective, and high return-on-investment. I have seen this process work magic in teams I have trained. The emails don't have to be long or flowery. The expectations are for simple, honest, heartfelt statements. Statements like these:

"Susan, I love the way you brighten my day with your bright smile'.

'Andrew, thank you for being someone I can always count on to deliver'.

Susan and Andrew now feel the affirmation that they are being noticed. They are happy.

Many companies have dedicated huddle times to set business goals and strategize. I would encourage a separate weekly huddle time for gratitude. A gratitude huddle is not just a feel-good time. People use this time to share challenges that came up from the week and also acknowledge how their colleagues helped them get through the challenges.

Having a whiteboard where people can write thank you notes for their colleagues is a simple way to kick-start the gratitude movement at work. Short, simple, heartfelt one-liners work just as well as longer ones. Make sure you do this without any physical or emotional expectations though.

Try an appreciation day at work. Not the kind where you choose someone to appreciate and everyone rallies around, or the kind of day where HR gives away freebies to thank you for your services. This appreciation day will be about everyone making a conscious effort to appreciate everyone they run into- with the expectation that this comes from a place of authenticity. We will always be able to find something wonderful about others if we put aside our judgments.

Do not miss opportunities to let your people know they are appreciated, especially when there is a dynamism in talent flow. This short fable reminds us to treat our existing people well:

A flock of beautiful swans landed on a field to rest. The farmer seeing how beautiful the swans were, went to the leader of the flock and tried to convince him to stay in his field.

"I will take good care of you," said the farmer, "you will get the choices of grains and the run of my field."

"Do you have other birds in your field?" asked the leader of the swans

"Yes, we have Geese."

"Where will they stay if we move in? What will they get to eat if we take the choicest of grains?"

"The geese will have to adjust." replied the farmer.

At this, the leader swan laughed.

"Next year, there may be a flock of peacocks landing in your field, and then we will become irrelevant. Why would we want to stay with someone who cannot appreciate what he already has? As for your geese, I would advise them to leave your field as soon as possible and find a patron who can be grateful for his flock."

With that, the swan and his flock flew away, never to return.

Another gratitude kickstarter is volunteering for people who have less than us. Exposure to want can help experience gratitude. Consider volunteering as a team for social causes that expose you to suffering. When the inner transformation to gratitude happens, and your colleagues are part of the gratitude journey, the sense of connection in workplaces is deepened. Many organizations have made it mandatory for their employees to volunteer their time for social causes of their choice.

Here is a simple on-the-go gratitude exercise to add to your daily routine. I call this the **3-2-1 gratitude method**. Think of

3 things you are thankful for about yourself

2 people you are thankful to

1 action point to express gratitude

This simple method rewires the brain to feel good about yourself and your community and creates accumulating changes.

Promoting gratitude as an influencer in your workplace

As an influencer and leader, you set the tone for gratitude in your workplace. Here are some questions to consider:

- Do I lead by example?
- Is my gratitude agnostic to job titles? In other words, is there a difference in how I thank someone who is positionally below me as opposed to someone above me?
- Am I sincere with thanks? One of the easiest ways to destroy trust is to be insincere with gratitude. If you thank me for being a great contributor to the team and shortly thereafter refuse to honor my request to leave early for a

medical procedure, I will likely question why you even thanked me in the first place.

- Does my gratitude come with an agenda? Agenda kills gratitude. If you thank with expectation, people will only see you as conniving. If you leverage your thanks as a way to get more work done, you lose trust.

- When does my gratitude happen? When gratitude is a knee jerk reaction, people see the gratitude as being sincere. Thank people at every opportunity and thank spontaneously.

- Is my gratitude just a verbal exercise? Tie your gratitude into the bigger picture of the person's happiness experience. If your gratitude does not empower me, I may feel disinclined to attach much value to your gratitude. The message is to make gratitude less transactional and more meaningful.

- Do I create opportunities for expressions of gratitude? Put up a gratitude board, encourage gratitude email strings, create gratitude huddles- anything that keeps the idea of being noticed and valued in plain sight.

Gratitude helps us think and act compassionately in both personal and professional settings. What are some steps I can do as an influencer in my current job setting to promote gratitude?

_____

_____

_____

_____

_____

_____

_____

_____

_____

_____

MY KEY TAKEAWAYS FROM THIS SECTION

SECTION 3:
COMPASSION EXPERIMENTS

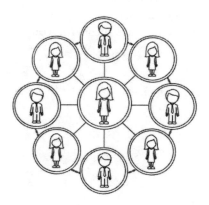

Exploring the 9-Pillars
of workplace compassion

"Today is a new day. Don't let your history interfere with your destiny! Let today be the day that you stop being a victim of your circumstances and start taking action towards the life you want. You have the power and the time to shape your life. Break free from the poisonous victim mentality and embrace the truth of your greatness. You were not meant for a mundane or mediocre life!"
— **Steve Maraboli**

Review of the 9-Pillars

The previous two sections of this book have hopefully made a case that compassion is a powerful antidote to the challenges you are experiencing in your workplace and that the practice of compassion is going to elevate your game to a whole new level. Now that you have all the compassion tools you need, it is time to experiment with them.

Before we explore implementation, here is a quick review of the 9-pillars and what it could mean for you individually and for your workplace.

	PILLAR	LACK LEADS TO	PERSONAL OUTCOMES	WORKPLACE OUTCOMES
1	Self compassion	Disruptive self criticism	Growth, freedom, Peace	Resilience, less burnout
2	People first	Misplaced priorities	Effective Leadership	Psychological safety, engagement
3	Abundance	Scarcity, hoarding	Openness, Generosity	Collaboration, resource sharing
4	Mindfulness	Stress, mind wandering	Balance, Peace	Presence, engagement
5	Oneness	Focus on differences	Human connection, Strong Relationships	Welcoming of diversity and inclusion
6	Appreciating Differences	Misplaced Expectation	Seeing others perspectives	Better Communication
7	Vulnerability	Fear	Authenticity, Courage	Trust, less conflict
8	Big picture	Lack of perspective & purpose	Perspective and purpose	Higher engagement, innovation
9	Gratitude	Entitlement	Acceptance, Happiness	Feeling valued, deeper connections, less stress

Experiments with the 9-Pillars

To start, let's revisit at some of the workplace challenges we saw in pages 33-42.

The exercise here is to experiment with how we can apply the 9-pillars as tools to address each of these workplace challenges. As you explore each of these scenarios, ask yourself this question: 'In my current situation, what is the most compassionate thing I can do?'

There are no correct or incorrect responses. You can choose to use any and all of the 9-pillars to address the suffering. Another fun thing to do is to explore compassion responses to these scenarios as a group or team activity in your workplace. I have given my interpretations for a couple of situations below.

Bias

The back-story:

Adhya comes from a conservative Indian background. She recently started working in a large IT company in San Francisco. She leads a small team of 12 people. One of her team members is Adam. Adam is gay. He is open about this fact. Adhya, because of her conservative upbringing, sees Adam's sexual preference as morally unacceptable. Even though she is trying to keep her views private, it shows up in how she judges Adam or treats him when things are not going well.

Response

Let's say Adhya asks the compassion check question:

'What is the compassionate thing to do when it comes to Adam?'

Adhya might remember that the very definition of compassion requires her to suspend judgment and that if her interactions with Adam have to be compassionate, she has to work on her own judgments about sexual preferences.

To help her with crafting a compassion response, Adhya might choose to reach out to her big-picture pillar. Big-picture thinking encourages her to see life from others' perspectives. Seeing through Adam's eyes, she might notice the suffering that she is inflicting on Adam with her biases. She might use the Oneness pillar to reflect that inclusion extends into the sexual preferences of the people she works with. She might decide to make mindful pauses before her interactions with Adam to make sure she is compassion-centered, and her biases do not show, even as she is working on taming them.

Gossiping at work

The back-story:

Beatrice recently started working as a teacher's aide in a special needs school. Beatrice is cheerful, talkative, and quickly connects with people. Sharon, another teacher's aide in a different classroom, is going through a difficult relationship with her supervising teacher. She has chosen to keep this to herself for several reasons. One day, when Beatrice and Sharon are alone in the lunchroom, Sharon opens up about her challenges to Beatrice and requests her to keep it confidential. Two weeks later, Sharon's supervising teacher confronts Sharon about her talking behind her back. Sharon knows that Beatrice must have told others about their private conversation. Sharon is angry and upset that Beatrice broke her trust.

Response:

Let's say Sharon asks herself the compassion question:

What is the compassionate thing to do for myself, for the situation and my colleagues?

Instead of becoming defensive, Sharon can come to accept that it was not the wisest decision to gossip about her supervisor. She could have addressed the situation directly with her boss instead of complaining to Beatrice. Nevertheless, since this is in the past, Sharon has to find ways to move forward.

As a first step, Sharon can reach for the self-compassion pillar in her tool belt. Self-compassion can help Sharon remember that imperfection is part of our shared human experience. With that clarity, she could use her vulnerability pillar and have an open dialogue with her supervisor. Sharon could admit that a mistake was indeed done, but also use this as an opportunity to broach the underlying problems between her and her supervisor. Her vulnerability can be the start of healing and the beginning of a new relationship with her supervisor.

Sharon might choose to have a vulnerable conversation with Beatrice, depending on their ongoing mutual levels of engagement. Sharon could choose to be self-compassionate and forgive Beatrice, but also making sure that she is reducing further opportunities to be hurt by her colleague.

Easily triggered

The back-story: Carter is branch manager for a large supermarket chain. He takes his work very seriously. He is very detail-oriented and works very hard to ensure that his branch has no customer complaints. He has a zero-tolerance policy for mistakes by the employees in his branch. Even small infractions are met with very tough responses. In the past, employees have been fired ungraciously by Carter for workplace errors, or have quit after yelling matches with Carter. No one questions Carter's commitment to the success of his branch, but his brusque personality and unwillingness to provide leeway for even the smallest mistakes makes him unpopular. Carter justifies that emotions do not have a role in the workplace.

Response

Many times, it takes a crisis for people to start looking for alternate solutions. Carter has to first buy into the idea that a compassion response is important for his workplace. Assuming that Carter is open to change, and is, in fact, asking the compassion question, 'What is the compassionate thing for me to do as a manager?', here are some ideas.

The two most important pillars that Cater needs to access in his tool kit are Big-picture and People first thinking. Big-picture thinking will help him re-evaluate his behavior in the context of his legacy. It will also help him see that winning small battles is not going to help him win the war. Also, people-first thinking will reinforce the importance of treating people not as resources, but as evolving assets. This could help him becoming more accepting of flaws in his teams and taking on a more human approach to business success.

Now, some work for you.

Which of the 9-Pillars can you apply in your current work setting? What is your game plan for using those pillars?

Challenge to address

Pillars to use

How I will use the pillar(s)

Expected outcome

How it played out

_____

_____

_____

_____

Creating compassion habits

Why do many motivational programs fail?

We learn, we are inspired, we act on the teaching for a few days. Then life happens. Other priorities take over. Even with the best of beginnings, learnings become meaningless if they do not become habits.

We are creatures of habit. We are capable of developing incredible behavioral patterns with habits. This story (source not known), although not about compassion, illustrates the point.

A wealthy businessman wanted to create a private zoo of exotic animals. He heard about a type of gazelle in Africa that was so fast that no one had ever succeeded in capturing it alive. Determined to include these gazelles in his collection, he traveled to the part of Africa where these gazelles lived. He tried to recruit the local hunters to capture the gazelles, but the answer was always the same- the gazelles were nocturnal, too wary, and too fast. The businessman said that he would catch the animals himself, without their help. The next day he set up a tent far away from the place where the gazelles were known to frequent at night. He made balls of grass and jaggery, which he had heard that all deer like to eat, and placed it near the gathering spot of the gazelle. Then he went back to his tent and watched. The first night, the gazelles came saw the unusual balls of food on the ground and ran away. The businessman repeated this the next day, and the next, but the gazelles refused to even come near the food. Finally, on the seventh day, one of the gazelles came and sniffed the food balls. He licked, then ate some of it, while the others in his flock watched. The following day a few more tried out the food balls, and soon after, every member of the herd was fighting to get to the food.

A week later, the businessman brought a plank of wood, about 2 meters tall, and stood it next to the food. That night, some of the deer saw the plank and hesitated, but seeing that some of their friends were getting the food without coming to harm, they decided to ignore the plank and eat the food. The following day, the businessman stood another plank right next to one before. He did this every single day, slowly laying out the planks in a circle around the food. After the first couple of days, the gazelles ignored the planks and were only worried about who was getting to the food first. Finally, there was space for just one more plank to complete the circle. The final night, the gazelles came for their food as usual. Seeing how narrow the opening was to get to their food, they jostled with each other to get into the enclosure where the food was. When the last of the gazelles were in, the businessman came running from his tent with the last plank and nailed it to the opening. That was it. All the gazelles were now trapped. The next morning, the businessman went to his enclosure, picked the ones that he wanted to keep and let the others go. The ones he chose, he transported to his private zoo in his native country, where they lived out the rest of their lives in captivity.

A 2009 study of rats found that, under chronic stress, they were much more likely to rely on automatic decisions (decisions we make purely through habit) than conscious ones they had clearly thought through[1]. Their brain compositions also changed to reflect this. The scientists behind this discovery think that it is about brain energy: in times of serious stress, the brain will take the easiest path, and expend as little energy as possible on making decisions, so it'll revert to habits. Charles Duhigg, author of the groundbreaking book, 'The Power of Habit', talks about the 'habit loop'. A habit loop starts with Cues. A cue must inspire an action, which should become a Routine. Routines must be paired with Rewards to incentivize action. The habit loop happens because our brains are plastic (as the Hebb's rule states, neurons that fire together, wire together) and there is a complex neurochemistry of risk and reward (as discussed in pages 10 to 16 by Dr. Breuning) that is happening under the surface.

Let me use an example from my life that has worked.

I have never been good at exercising. I have tried taking gym memberships many times only to cancel them because of non-use. A year ago, I started to experiment with habits. I looked at my day and realized that I spend quite a bit of time at the microwave. I also noticed that I almost always spend the waiting time stimming on my phone. I decided that I would use the waiting time to exercise-pushups, pullups, sit-ups, or some quick, intense physical activity. This was inspired by Tabata workouts, which involve just 4 minutes of high intensity working out, and is more impactful than a control medium intensity training regimen.

So, in my habit experiment, every time I put something in the microwave, I would exercise until the end 'ding' happened. I went through phases- I did well the first few days, then I flaked out, but then I restarted- but I persisted. But since these were short bursts of action with a clear endpoint, it was doable. I also noticed that internally, I was able to push through the exercises knowing that a cup of tea or hot food was waiting at the end of the activity. This was my reward. Thus, I had set up my habit loop. The start of a microwave was my cue to exercise. The exercise was part of my routine. And hot food at the end of the exercise was my reward. To date, this is the most effective exercise regimen I have taken on.

Another powerful habit-forming method that works is the power of unfinished tasks.

The Zeigarnik effect is a psychological bias that was described in 1927 by Bluma Zeigarnik[2]. It came from observations that a waiter could remember orders as long as they were unpaid, but could not recollect the details of the orders after the bills had been settled. The Zeigarnik effect states that people tend to remember unfinished tasks better than finished tasks. This bias has been put to good use in dealing with procrastination challenges. For example, if we have a 30-page project that is due in a month, according to the Zeigarnik effect, it would be a good idea to start today, even if it means investing only 15 minutes of rough sketching the project outline. Because the project is now started and unfinished, the brain will tend to pester you to return to the task and complete it. We can apply the habit-loop and Zeigarnik effect in forming principles in compassion skilling our organizations and ourselves.

What is one compassion habit you want to build in your life? What are some of the most tangible expressions of that habit? What can be a Cue to remind you to put that habit into practice consistently? How will you reward yourself when you practice that habit?

_____

_____

_____

_____

_____

_____

_____

_____

_____

_____

_____

_____

The 9-Pillars Mantra

Personally, one of the daily cues I use to practice everyday compassion is the **9-pillar mantra**. I have this little card in my bathroom, which I get to read while I brush my teeth. This is how it goes.

May I practice compassion for myself without judgment

May I truly value and cherish the people I work with and serve

May I flourish in a mindset of abundance

May I be mindful of my thoughts, words and actions

May I embrace the diversity of races, cultures and personalities around me

May I communicate my compassion with conviction and clarity

May I be courageous to be vulnerable in the right circumstances

May I see my life and work with purpose and perspective

May I feel gratitude for all people, experiences and gifts in my life.

Bringing compassion practices to teams

Once you have nailed down your compassion habits, you can set your eyes on transforming your workplace; you can inspire the compassion shift and create compassionate cultures.

When you have honed in on the desire to help nudge your team toward compassion, just start! There is no perfect time to start. Set the ball in motion. Allow the Zeigarnik effect to propel you toward a clearly defined goal. Today, simply draw out the to-do list for compassion skilling your team or organization. Tomorrow you will find yourself pulled toward executing on one step in your to-do list. The day after there will be one more reason to come to it. Before you know it, you would have made enough headway and gained enough clarity to step into tangible action. And that is how, as a compassion leader, you become the change, one step at a time.

You do not have to be a team or group leader to make these shifts, but it helps if you have the buy-in and support of leadership to make this happen. It is important to remember that not everyone in your circle is going to see value in the idea of deliberately creating compassionate work cultures. I believe there is a rough bell curve distribution: the ends of the bell curve are people who are bought into compassion and people who will never buy into compassion. The majority of people, those who form the center of the curve, are unsure. They are waiting for permission and proof. When the permission comes from leadership, and proof comes from colleagues, they happily follow along. Of course, they will look around to see if there is a social consensus, but eventually, they will become compassion yes-sayers. Your task as a compassion evangelist, whatever your role in the organization, is to introduce the topic, hammer away at the resistance, and facilitate the change.

For example, in your team meeting, you could introduce the idea of compassion through visioning. As a team, work on these questions:

- How would a compassionate workplace look like?
- What problems in your current work setting would a culture of compassion solve?
- What would it take to make that change?
- If the workplace were compassionate, what would the pulse feel like (feelings/ actions/ tangible behaviors)?
- What would every individual's role in creating this environment be?

Compassion Hackathons

People love solutions that they were involved in creating. That is why I created the idea of **compassion hackathons**. Hacking means breaking into. Traditional hackathons are where people come together to hack into problems and co-create solutions. Compassion hackathons are not very different. In compassion hackathons, people come together to lay out their organizational or team problems and co-create solutions using the 9-pillars as a framework. It is an elegant, powerful, and incredibly fun experience. In our work, we follow this up with technology-based reinforcements, and strategic challenges and check-ins to cement the transformation. By itself, though, a compassion hackathon is a powerful hands-on experience for attendees. We start with the commitment that every hackathon creates solutions that are *Effective, Measurable, and Practical*. Here is a simple outline I use for conducting compassion hackathons.

Hackathon Rules

EMP
EFFECTIVE-MEASURABLE-PRACTICAL

Problem:
Create a technology or human solution for a problem using the 9-pillars of workplace compassion framework

Process:
1. Form teams
2. Choose a challenge (eg improving employee collaboration, improving interpersonal skill sharing, boosting innovative thinking, Improving loyalty, etc.)
3. Brainstorm
4. Create
5. Present (5 minutes)

Some Considerations—
1. Who is your target?
2. How is your product unique?
3. Why will people use your product?
4. How will you drive sustained usage?
5. What is the opportunity for expansion?
6. What are the biggest anticipated objections?
7. What resources will you need?
8. How will you measure the effectiveness of your solution?

Great ideas appear and solidify during compassion hackathons. For example, during one of the compassion hackathons I was conducting, Western Dentistry (name changed), a 12 people dental office, discovered that there was a general lack of appreciation in the practice. As a team, Western Dentistry decided that going forward, the entire team would meet for a gratitude huddle. The huddles were going to be half-hour events, which, unlike their other planning huddles which happened every morning, would be about showing gratitude for the others, and addressing any blocks that came in the way of appreciating others (for example, conflicts because of overscheduling, customer issues). One of the team members became the cheerleader for this project. She started leaving small pink sticky notes reminding people of the gratitude huddle and adding little positive messages to the notes. These sticky notes became cues for the team, not just to attend the huddle, but also to also remember to appreciate each other through the rest of the week. The owner of the dentistry decided to incentivize attendance by conducting it during business hours and sponsoring pizza and drinks for the huddle. A nice habit loop formed for the team. Pink sticky notes in the office became cues for gratitude, the huddle was the routine where people worked actively on the issue, and the food and drinks were the rewards, although happily this was overtaken by the genuine feelings of warmth and connection that were created during the huddle.

What is one compassion habit my team can create? What will the Cues, Routines, and Rewards of our compassion habit look like?

_____

_____

_____

_____

_____

_____

_____

_____

_____

_____
_____
_____
_____
_____
_____

Introducing compassion programs
in organizations

Change is never easy. It takes strategy and persistence to be a compassion evangelist in your organization. If you have indeed taken on the task of being a compassion leader in your organization, here is a plan that might be useful for you.

Introducing a compassion program in my company

Whose buy-in do I need?

Who will evangelize this cause?
PHASE I PLANNING
Who are my key supporters?

Who are my critics?
Who are my collaborators?

Who will I internally market my program to?

How can I create successive programs?
PHASE II IMPLEMENTATION
How will I internally market my program?

How will I measure success?
How will my beta program look like?

How will I scale up my program?

What is my legacy plan (hand over)?
PHASE III EXPANSION
How will I train other people to teach?

How will I access the needed resources?
What technology support will I need?

I want to share some inspiring examples of people who dove in with passion and created change in their organizations.

Lindsay Benjamin
Mindfulness Lead, Intel Corporation, Oregon, USA

AWAKE is a 10-week mindfulness program at Intel that was started as a grassroots effort seven years ago by two Intel employees- Lindsay Benjamin and Quo Vade. The program has been extraordinarily successful. Intel is a 100,000 people company, distributed across the globe. Close to 5000 employees have already gone through the mindfulness training across their offices in the USA, Mexico, Costa Rica, and India. How can a grassroots vision of two individuals within an organization expand into a global program influencing thousands of employees?

Lindsay Benjamin shares her journey.

"I had been a mindfulness and yoga teacher for a long time. After I joined Intel, I was informally training mindfulness at the onsite gyms. So the passion was there. One day, my mother sent an article to me about Google's mindfulness training program. That, to me, was my' aha' moment. I knew then I had to bring mindfulness programs to Intel. When we first started seven years ago, it was just a proof of concept effort. 'Let's get some 20 engineers in the room and teach them basic mindfulness concepts'. But we did our training, and we got these profound results. At the end of the first proof of concept, the engineers who had been struggling with a specific problem were able to connect and solve the problem together. With those amazing results in hand, we started advertising locally- first within our campus and then across the other 4 Intel campuses in Oregon. We created an internal blog to share these stories and gauge interest. We found there was plenty of interest in our program. The employees loved it that they could put down their laptop and get centered during the workday on company time. Our program gave them a platform to work through some difficult emotions and stress, and because these challenges are so fundamental and prevalent in organizations, there was an endless demand for our program.

There's research from Harvard, which shows that 7-8 minutes of meditation a day for 8-weeks produces measurable changes in the brain. We structured our program for 10-weeks with a requirement that people who join commit to attending for at least eight weeks. We have not had a problem with people not following through on this commitment. To begin with, people who attend have self-selected to attend the program. People do genuinely love attending the training. To strengthen their commitment, we charge a 100-dollar fee for attendance, which pays for journals and books. But even that small financial investment creates a commitment to attend the full program. Also, employees are encouraged to buddy-up and share during the trainings. This builds trust and commitment to complete the 10-weeks. We celebrate completion with little gifts- mindfulness programs and resources to help them continue the practice.

By year three in the program, it became apparent that we needed to train more teachers. There were 4 of us teaching at that time, and we all had our day jobs to attend to. By this time, word about our program had gotten around, and Intel employees in California wanted the training as well. The high-tech industry, on the whole, does through the same suffering- work is fast-paced, there is lots of change and lots of competition. I had the help of a course designer from Intel- who helped me put the presentation together slide-by-slide. As soon as we had this resource, it was easy to train trainers. We have to be careful in choosing our trainers. Our trainers are people who have typically had at least 1000 hours of meditation practice and are deeply passionate about teaching. But wherever we look, and wherever we ask, we always find a few people who fit the bill perfectly. That is all we need really- just a couple of teachers per site who are genuinely passionate.

For a mindfulness program to be attractive, it has to have applicability to work. This is what makes the business case and generate support for these programs. In my case, I certainly knew how to teach mindfulness, but it took me 2 or 3 iterations before I could bridge the gaps in terms of applicability. From the beginning, we made sure that we would measure the effectiveness of the training with assessments. We also made it easy for people to share their experiences in the program as anecdotal feedback. We have had some amazing stories come out of it. People share how mindfulness has helped them deal with losses, helps them get through divorces, or find a better job match. For example, we recently had one attendee share this: "I have much better emotional regulation because of mindfulness training. I find I am now able to not take on others' emotions. As a result, for the first time in 8 years, I have stopped taking high blood pressure medication." It's nice when we have physical evidence like that for a training program.

For people who are planning to start something like this in their organizations, here are a couple of pointers. Starting a program like this does not have to be a top-down approach. We took our idea to management- expressed what we wanted to do and why and made a business case, and they were ok with it. Then HR got involved, and they audited us, and we were able to grow. My advice to people who want to do something similar is to be absolutely clear about what you are offering, what your expected outcomes are, and how that ties to their business. If you are leveraging the businesses' resources, they need to see value in making it happen. If mindfulness is already in the psyche of the organization, then it's easy for an employee to get the support to build an internal program. If you have a clear vision, talk to your manager, talk to your HR, and be prepared to show how you will measure impact. Once you have the buy-in, test it. Run a proof of concept. See what happens; see what's good and what's not. Treat it like a startup. Get feedback. Iterate. Tweak it until it feels right for you as the teacher.

That's how successful programs are launched and implemented." **"**

Being a force of good

As you probably are thinking now, becoming a compassion leader in your organization may not be an easy journey. The question that may come up is, **"Why should I even undertake this difficult path of being a change-maker in my organization?"**

The truth is, being a change-maker is not for everyone. It is an inner calling, which becomes louder and louder and will not rest until it is addressed. This calling prompts us to take risks and become voices of change when everyone else around us is silent. That calling and how we heed to them is what makes leaders. But more than anything else, knowing that our efforts to lead with compassion in our workplaces is making a human impact for our colleagues, is priceless. I believe we are all meant to shine and soar, even if the paths are rough. This is what will make the stories of our lives meaningful.

'A ship in harbor is safe, but that is not what ships are built for' — **John Shedd**.

Once a compassion program is created, it is important that it be allowed to percolate through all layers of the organization. Most organizations have clear values guidelines, but many do not have a clear strategy to follow through. Here is an example, where a company's values program actually translated into compassion in the face of suffering?

Realizing the importance of being a force of good as an organization, VMWare created its EPIC2 program. EPIC2 is VMWare's values guideline that is an acronym for Execution, Passion, Integrity, Customers, and Community. The focus on customers and community is taken seriously. While most companies have ambitious values guidelines, some companies do not take the effort to actively implement their program. VMWare however, has been successful in ensuring that all its employees across the globe are bought into the values program. New hires to VMWare are reinforced with EPIC2 values at their time of entry. The values are continually reinforced during quarterly meetings. The company encourages its employees to give back (skills, time, or other efforts) to their communities, and has a peer-nomination system to reward extraordinary acts of human kindness at all-hands meetings.

More importantly, as **Grant Nowell, IT Operations Manager at VMWare** points out, a program like this is successful because all layers of leadership, including the CEO of VMWare, model the values in real life. This includes creating a layer of flexibility in work- making sure that adversity is met with appropriate opportunities for alleviation. For example, Grant tells the story of a colleague who suffered kidney failure, and the team leaders and colleagues made sure that he was given the space and time to recover, and could work from home at a pace that met his health needs- while making sure that his value and role in the company were untarnished. Because of the ever-prevalent emphasis on the compassionate side of business, employees at all levels of the organization feel empowered to practice compassion when suffering strikes.

Case in point: Grant's team in India lost a release manager to heart failure. The response from VMWare's leadership and colleagues was quick and effective. They created a global fundraising initiative to support the family of the deceased, which is fairly standard for most companies. Not stopping with fundraising however, they made sure that colleagues were available to support the grieving family, often physically present to handle the challenges of the departure of the sole breadwinner in the family, and periodically checking in to ensure the family's well being. The physical presence and timeliness of the support was an act of compassion that really made a positive impact on the family of the deceased. Noticing that the surviving widow, who was at that time a home-maker, was qualified to become a teacher, the team members used their collective network to find her a position as a teacher in a local school, thereby ensuring her wellbeing would extend far beyond a traditional knee jerk response to suffering. In addition, noticing that the mother of the deceased colleague was sick and needed medical help, they arranged for proper medical care for her.

This experience from Grant Nowell's team is a good example of how organizational value systems if properly communicated and implemented, can translate into human action in the face of suffering. If this compassion response seems somewhat similar to Chandra Elango's story on page Introduction, it is because Chandra's experience preceded Grant's experience with his team, and in some ways became an inspiration for compassionate responses within the company in the face of incredible tragedy. This again is a beautiful example of how compassion can have ripple effects within organizations.

Measuring success of compassion programs

One of the first lessons you learn during a Ph.D. in science is that if it cannot be measured, it does not exist. That is true of compassion programs as well. If you are taking your field-tested program to your leaders for support and expansion, you will need to show significant numbers. At the very least, you should be able to demonstrate proof that a significant percentage of people in your organization agree with you.

Mandar Apte
Peace Activist, Executive Director of From India with Love.

"In 2012, I had joined the Gamechanger program within Shell. This is a program that helps foster innovation by investing in people with extraordinary ideas. I felt that innovation is more of a social than a technical process. For successful innovation, we must not only invest money, but also invest in developing their social and mental skills. I communicated my vision to my supervisor and got his buy-in. The company made arrangements so that I could spend 10% of my time teaching meditation to foster innovation within the company. With this support, I could bring my personal passion for teaching meditation and mindfulness to the workplace to boost innovation.

We made some smart decisions at the very beginning. One, this would not be a mandatory top-down program, and two, it would be employee-driven, i.e., employees would organize these trainings for other employees. Self-election is a critical component for the success of a program like this. Because they are responding to an invitation from a colleague, employees who attend are more open to the learnings from the program. People typically attend meditation programs out of curiosity or health issues. But wrapping our program as an innovation booster added to the interest and success. We measured our success with three simple self-reporting questions:

Was this program a good use of your time?

Would you recommend this program to a colleague?

Has this program resulted in you interacting with at least one other colleague to create an innovative idea?

The program has taken by more than 2000 employees at Shell. We have received 97-98% positive responses to these questions. So we knew we were on the right track.

What we have learned is, if we provide something that people love, they will naturally share it. That is how programs like these spread and grow. That is how cultural movements within organizations are created."

Here is *one of the assessments I use* for measuring baselines and shifts of compassion behaviors in workplaces. This particular assessment is part of a dyad used for measuring compassion among colleagues.

Compassion Assessment

Instructions

This survey intends to help you understand the relationship dynamics in your workplace.

Please respond to the questions below by circling the answer that most resonates with you.

Assessment

I notice when my colleagues are going through challenges.

Totally disagree	Somewhat disagree	Neither agree or disagree	Somewhat agree	Totally agree

2. My colleagues feel comfortable opening up to me about their challenges.

Totally disagree	Somewhat disagree	Neither agree or disagree	Somewhat agree	Totally agree

3. I have a positive relationship with time. I see time as a friend, not as a threat.

Totally disagree	Somewhat disagree	Neither agree or disagree	Somewhat agree	Totally agree

4. If I make a mistake at work, I feel safe owning it.

Totally disagree	Somewhat disagree	Neither agree or disagree	Somewhat agree	Totally agree

5. I have clarity about the bigger goals of my organization and my role in achieving it.

Totally disagree	Somewhat disagree	Neither agree or disagree	Somewhat agree	Totally agree

6. I do not judge my colleagues because of their personal situations.

Totally disagree	Somewhat disagree	Neither agree or disagree	Somewhat agree	Totally agree

7. In general, our workplace uses inclusive 'We' statements more than 'I' statements.

Totally disagree	Somewhat disagree	Neither agree or disagree	Somewhat agree	Totally agree

8. I earnestly try to help my colleagues resolve their problems.

Totally disagree	Somewhat disagree	Neither agree or disagree	Somewhat agree	Totally agree

9. I feel motivated to show up on time and deliver my tasks on time.

Totally disagree	Somewhat disagree	Neither agree or disagree	Somewhat agree	Totally agree

10. I take feelings into consideration when I correct a colleague's mistake.

Totally disagree	Somewhat disagree	Neither agree or disagree	Somewhat agree	Totally agree

11. I feel valued as a person at work.

Totally disagree	Somewhat disagree	Neither agree or disagree	Somewhat agree	Totally agree

12. My colleagues communicate with kindness.

Totally disagree	Somewhat disagree	Neither agree or disagree	Somewhat agree	Totally agree

13. I feel a positive sense of connection with my colleagues.

Totally disagree	Somewhat disagree	Neither agree or disagree	Somewhat agree	Totally agree

14. I feel motivated to give the best of my skills to my role.

Totally disagree	Somewhat disagree	Neither agree or disagree	Somewhat agree	Totally agree

15. I feel that love, not fear, drives my relationship with my boss and colleagues.

Totally disagree	Somewhat disagree	Neither agree or disagree	Somewhat agree	Totally agree

16. I believe I contribute positively to strong workplace connections.

Totally disagree	Somewhat disagree	Neither agree or disagree	Somewhat agree	Totally agree

17. My organization honors and empowers my need for personal growth.

Totally disagree	Somewhat disagree	Neither agree or disagree	Somewhat agree	Totally agree

18. As an individual, I feel I have the skill sets to handle conflict effectively.

Totally disagree	Somewhat disagree	Neither agree or disagree	Somewhat agree	Totally agree

19. When I encounter differences of opinion at work, I have the skills to handle them gracefully.

Totally disagree	Somewhat disagree	Neither agree or disagree	Somewhat agree	Totally agree

20. I perceive my organization as a compassionate place, where people genuinely care for people.

Totally disagree	Somewhat disagree	Neither agree or disagree	Somewhat agree	Totally agree

21. I believe I can keep the work focus while still being compassionate.

Totally disagree	Somewhat disagree	Neither agree or disagree	Somewhat agree	Totally agree

22. I am able to see past the social and cultural differences of my colleagues.

Totally disagree	Somewhat disagree	Neither agree or disagree	Somewhat agree	Totally agree

23. My workplace makes me want to give my best to work.

Totally disagree	Somewhat disagree	Neither agree or disagree	Somewhat agree	Totally agree

24. My organization communicates its vision to us effectively.

Totally disagree	Somewhat disagree	Neither agree or disagree	Somewhat agree	Totally agree

25. I feel that my management treats me fairly.

Totally disagree	Somewhat disagree	Neither agree or disagree	Somewhat agree	Totally agree

26. My organization recognizes and rewards me appropriately for the work I do.

Totally disagree	Somewhat disagree	Neither agree or disagree	Somewhat agree	Totally agree

27. My organization operates with an abundance mindset. My organization encourages sharing of skills and resources.

Totally disagree	Somewhat disagree	Neither agree or disagree	Somewhat agree	Totally agree

28. I am inspired to be a better person because I work here.

Totally disagree	Somewhat disagree	Neither agree or disagree	Somewhat agree	Totally agree

29. I am comfortable about the prospects of my career growth in my current role.

Totally disagree	Somewhat disagree	Neither agree or disagree	Somewhat agree	Totally agree

30. My company is considerate with my work expectations and deadlines.

Totally disagree	Somewhat disagree	Neither agree or disagree	Somewhat agree	Totally agree

Additional comments

_____

_____

_____

_____

_____

_____

_____

_____

Creating supportive frameworks for compassion

Leading people may not always be easy, but the payback is that we get to influence so many lives. 72% of employees are highly engaged in organizations with effective leadership[3]. As a leader who leads with compassion, you are uniquely positioned to bring happiness and balance into your organization. But it can be challenging to go it alone as a compassion leader.

One of the things you would want to ensure, if you have the influence to do so, is to put into place systems and processes to recruit people with a propensity for compassion into your organization. One of the ways you can do this is by asking for specific examples of compassion from their previous jobs during the interview process. You can look at the content of their answers, but also weigh the spontaneity of the answers, whether there was offered to someone higher or lower than them positionally, etc. You could use behavioral tags and assessments to screen for compassionate behaviors during recruiting, in essence letting your potential recruits know that you are serious about compassionate behaviors should they become part of the organization. Conversely, it is important to recognize that everybody wants to work for compassionate leaders. Larger organizations could consider including a compassion rating for leaders, which can be made available as necessary to employees moving into new teams. You can be the leader bringing the compassion change to your organization. It may be difficult, but it can be done.

'Change cannot be put on people. The best way to instill change is to do it with them. Create it with them.'
— **Lisa Bodell**

MY KEY TAKEAWAYS FROM THIS SECTION

_____

_____

_____

_____

_____

_____

_____

_____

_____

_____

_____

_____

_____

_____

_____

_____

_____

_____

_____

SECTION 4:
A SYSTEMS APPROACH
TO COMPASSION

Societies
Governments
Organizations

COMPASSION

Self-Compassion | People First | Abundance | Mindfulness | Oneness | Differences | Vulnerability | Big Picture | Gratitude

Thus far in the book, we have discussed compassion in workplaces, compassion skills to use to shift ourselves and the people we influence. In this section, we will explore how we can scale up compassion to create cultural shifts at the levels of organizations and governments. We will also delve into how we can skill-up for a compassionate future.

Creating compassionate cultural umbrellas

'Culture is simply a shared way of doing something with a passion.'
— **Brian Chesky, Co-Founder, CEO, Airbnb**

I like to think of culture as the soil in which our human potential can thrive or perish. Sadly, Only 28% of executives believe they understand their company culture and only 12% of executives believe their companies are driving the right culture[1]. If the culture of our organization does not permit or support it, we will never be able to fully apply our passion for compassion at work. After all, even the hardiest of plants fail to bloom when they are not in the right soil. Similarly, for its individuals to be effective and successful, the organization must also cultivate the right environment for the 'human' behind the employee to flourish. Creating an organizational culture of productivity and caring is an effort that involves the participation of everyone in the organization. From the CEO to Janitor, the onus is on every individual in the organization to create a collective culture that values its people and nurtures trust, psychological safety, care, support, and happiness. When this kind of culture is manifested, it can be a powerful magnet for talent retention and engagement.

How intimate are you with your company's culture?
If your company were a person, how would you describe her?
For example, is she kind, generous, empowering, safe, civil,
considerate, authentic, honest, caring?

_____

_____

_____

_____

_____

_____

_____

_____

_____

_____

_____

_____

_____

_____

_____

_____

Look at your answers above. Consider that you have a role in
making your company the way you have described her. Reflect on
how you have contributed to the current cultural shape of your
organization.

Individuals and organizational cultures

Individuals shape culture, and reciprocally, culture shapes individuals, as illustrated in the image below.

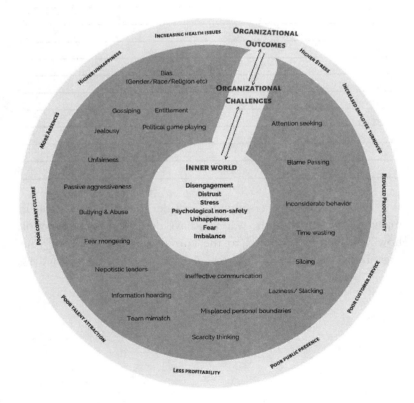

Grassroots efforts toward compassion must be paired with leadership support and resources for large scale shifts in culture to happen. In large organizations, cultural shift happens when there is a tipping point created by many teams moving toward the same goal of a compassionate workplace. How can we direct multiple teams to the same goal? This is where senior leadership sets the vision and creates opportunities for transformation to happen.

Shifting to compassionate cultures requires a multipronged approach.

Leaders create permissions, set the tone, and facilitate opportunities for creating a shift to compassion. They model the change they want to see.

Individuals get skilled in practical compassion, and in a grassroots format, become nodes for compassion skills training and application.

Throughout the organization, **'compassion moais'** form and support each other in the cultural shift. (Moais are support systems of friends in Okinawa, Japan. Members of moais are lifelong companions who make sure no member of their group suffers hardship or goes through loss alone. Moais are considered one of the reasons why parts of Okinawa report some of the longest lifespans in the world[2]).

Voila! We have an organization that lives and breathes compassion, and people who flourish in a compassionate culture.

Convincing your flock to follow you into compassion requires *strategy*.

There is a Sunday school story about a shepherd who was trying to get his flock to cross a stream. The sheep were afraid and refused to cross. Finally, the shepherd picked up a tiny lamb, and holding it tight, began to cross the stream. The mother ewe hearing the voice of her baby, braved the water and started following the shepherd across the stream. Seeing one of their flock crossing the water, the other members of the flock began crossing the stream one by one, until every one of them reached the other side.

As leaders model change, others follow. Here is an example:

Trish Stevens
Ascot Media

"**M**any years ago, I was an Executive Assistant at Continental Airlines Corporate Office. A new CEO (Gordon Bethune) came on board and changed everything—instantly! The first thing he changed was how management was towards employees, and vice versa. "Dignity and Respect" went into action immediately, and for anyone that didn't abide by those rules—were out! Well, my boss went from being "mean and ungrateful" to "amazing, complementary and joyful" overnight. In fact, he became the best boss I had ever had. I absolutely loved working for him. Compassion automatically went hand-in-hand with dignity and respect. We instantly saw each other in a whole new light and work, from that moment on, became a delight. I no longer dreaded walking into my office. All of us assistants became one big happy family, and we couldn't do enough for each other. Our jobs were wonderful, and our bosses were even better!"

It takes visionary leadership to break through the prevailing perception of hard business, create and sustain human-centric policies.

The small town of Bethel, Alaska, with only 6400 residents, received an extraordinary treat of Tacos in 2012. And it started with a hoax. Two residents of this little town, which is extraordinarily difficult to access, decided to spread a rumor that **TacoBell** was opening a branch in Bethel. Soon the hoax was discovered, but there was disappointment. The closest TacoBell is at Anchorage Alaska, 400 miles away. While the story could have ended there, TacoBell's CEO Greg Creed and his leadership team saw this as an opportunity for kindness. To counter the disappointment of their fans, TacoBell had a truck with ingredients for 10,000 Tacos- 950 pounds of beef, 500 pounds of sour cream, 300 pounds of tomatoes, 400 pounds of lettuce, and 105 pounds of cheddar cheese- airlifted to the town. People of Bethel were delighted! There are anecdotal stories that Taco Bell's compassion for Bethel's residents continued well past this incident, thanks to leadership who believed in the power of compassion over hard financial gains.

Another leader who has been a great evangelist of compassion in workplaces is **Jeff Weiner**, the founder of LinkedIn. Weiner shares that "managing compassionately is about putting yourself in another person's shoes and seeing the world through their lens or perspective." Putting this principle of compassion has made him one of the CEOs with consistently high approval ratings from employees. In summer 2019, LinkedIn a $100,000 compassion award to recognize individuals and organizations bringing compassion work to the world. Through the award, LinkedIn managed to create a platform for compassion leaders from across the globe to highlight their work and highlight conversations on compassion.

As good leadership fosters compassion and creates opportunities, bad leadership destroys opportunities through a lack of compassion. Consider the case of Hannah. Hannah used to be an Organic Chemist in a Biotech firm.

Hannah L,
Homemaker

"I worked as a chemist in a biotech company developing drugs. My team leader was one of the kindest, genuinely caring leaders I have ever met in my life. She took a personal interest in every single person in her team, making sure that we felt valued, safe and heard. Her authenticity and space she created for us to grow at our own pace, made us want to show up as the best versions of ourselves every day. Under her leadership, I felt I could voice opinions and take risks without being shot down. And we always prioritized science to personal ego. She created an environment where we wanted to shine, but also made sure she communicated her expectations clearly and held us accountable. This was valuable for me, since this was my first job outside of graduate school. This safe space and trust enabled me to innovate fearlessly. I ended up creating two new lines of research in my organization, publish papers, and create several industry-academia collaborations. I was a success. But more importantly, I was also very happy. This happiness reflected in my life outside work as well. I was building great social relationships in and out of work.

After more than four years of positives, we went through a company reorganization. My new team leader (let's call him Z) was a seasoned scientist, but came from a different research specialization. Even as he started heading our team, I felt the element of trust was missing. Z quickly forced out a long term team member and brought in his friend from his old team. Z was charming to talk to, a picture of kindness, but somehow, you sensed that there was little substance behind that facade. Ours was a hierarchical organization, so Z was the primary conduit to senior leadership. It took only a short while to realize that Z would not hesitate to throw you under the bus if it made him look good.

Slowly, as a team, our focus shifted from science to survival. This was the time of a difficult job market for the biotech industry. So team members were scrambling to keep their jobs. Z actively positioned people against each other in ways that shifted the power equation toward him. After Z came into our team, I lost my drive to innovate. I felt that I was not valued or trusted. I did not have a team to fall back on. Most of my office hours were now about doing the strategic thing that would still keep me relevant, and thus employed in my role. I hated every minute of going to work, but I had financial obligations to meet. I accomplished very little every day, and still, when I came home, I felt drained and unhappy. My personal life was suffering too.

The worst part? With constant belittling from Z, I was beginning to doubt my own capability as a scientist. Z made sure that he magnified my errors and refused to acknowledge my accomplishments, because as he said: "science is about poking holes until you get perfect solutions." But then, I came to know that he had taken credit from senior leadership for several of the ideas I had shared with him - the very same ideas he had shot down as 'not scientifically ready'. The final straw came when the projects that I had worked so hard to create were 'taken over' by Z because he felt that I had too many things on my plate. Even though I had some good friends in the company, I was stuck in cultural narratives that held me back from reaching out for help or advice. The two significant people in my support net, including my former team leader, had been let go. I remember I had a corner of my desk dedicated to drawing lines and crosses to mark the passing of days, like prisoners do in jail cells. When I finally left the organization, after seven months of enduring humiliation and self-doubt, I was depressed and lost my enthusiasm for science. And all it took was one bad leader to lose my love for science. **"**

Every change goes through phases of criticism, resistance, curiosity, experimentation, acceptance, expansion, and adoption. The call for a normalization of compassion in workplaces is such a basic human need, that the criticism and resistance are easily overcome. But the curiosity is lacking, and the true resistance you might meet is people seeing the value for compassion.

Imagine as an exercise that you are **the CEO (Chief Emotions Officer)** of your company. **What can you do in your visionary role to create a culture of compassion?**

When there is leadership willpower to promote compassion, organizations can become the force of change in their communities. Medical care is one of those areas where compassion is an in-built requirement. In medicine, we deal with frail, vulnerable people who come to us in the worst phase of their lives. It is not pretty dealing with disease and pain day after day. And in today's world where a doctor's bonus is tied to patient load and patient satisfaction, and the constant pressure to not be litigated against, caring for the sick becomes a delicate balancing act. It is easy to get burnt out; it is easy to be discompassionate and treat patients as numbers and not as human beings seeking our comfort. Hospitals are cognizant of the challenges that their providers are facing. Mindfulness programs are becoming increasingly common in hospitals. Some hospitals are getting their staff immersed in a culture of kindness, so they are able to meet the worst of their workplace with compassion for self and others.

One hospital system that has made kindness its cultural tenet is **Dignity Health** (now CommonSpirit Health). Dignity Health is the fifth largest healthcare system in the United States and operates hospitals and ancillary care facilities in three states. Dignity Health's slogan is *'Hello Humankindness'*, which was launched in 2013. The initiative was in part influenced by research from Dignity Health that showed that what people most want in a health care experience is to be listened to- to be treated as a person, not a patient. 'Hello Humankindness' also intends to remind people that while incivility may be all too common, acts of human kindness happen every day. As Llyod Dean, CEO of Dignity Health pointed out, "while medicine has the power to cure, it's humanity that holds the power to heal." Since the time of launch, Hello Humankindness' has become the face of DignityHealth. The campaign has tapped into the power of real human stories to inspire acts of kindness in the communities they serve. Dignity Health's kindness campaign inspires the question: What if more and more organizations made kindness and compassion as the face of their business?

Compassion as extension of our company's services

And it is not only the healthcare organizations that have opportunities to be a force of compassionate change in their communities. Wherever there is an opportunity to interface with our communities through our products or services, there is an opportunity to relieve suffering and practice compassion.

Arturo Bejar
Former Head of Engineering, Facebook

"Customer service is where pain goes to die. Several years ago, I inherited the customer care program at Facebook. We found that there were a number of issues, like people asking to remove certain postings on Facebook, but very little was being acted upon. Most had nothing to do with company policies, but had to do with negative human experiences. An example of this is when someone posts a photo of you that you do not like, but you do not want to confront that person directly for personal reasons, you complain to Facebook that the post has nudity hoping to make that image go away, when in fact there was no nudity. We began to understand that the issues we were dealing with had to do with how humans get along with each other in the world, carried over into a virtual platform.

Sitting at the Wisdom 2.0 conference in San Francisco, I head Jack Kornfield and Jon Kabat-Zinn discuss how, if we saw people as full human beings, having good days and bad days, we would engage with them differently. I made this connection that the way we can help people navigate difficult moments on our Facebook platform is by seeing them and hearing them, and then creating an experience which acknowledges challenges. In an incidence that involves two people, you could do one of two things: you could be a referee, which nobody likes, or you could help people connect with each other. So the question for me became 'How can we build the connection? How can we be of service to people's relationships in the world?'

Upfront, we realized this was not going to be a social program for the company. Social programs require sponsorship and funding. This was going to be about helping Facebook interface with its community through compassion.

We started with some essential questions.

"What is the suffering that is happening in the product we had created, when people connect with us because they need our help with something? Can we measure it? Can we share the measurements with other people?"

Our fundamental goal was helping people see each other. The specific challenge for my team was, 'How do you turn these principles into a pragmatic approach that can be measured?'

I never found resistance in the work I was doing, because Facebook cared about the community. People were having a difficult time. It was completely coherent for the corporation to help people who were having a difficult time. It was always our mission. We had a problem that needed to be addressed- that had to do with easing people's suffering on the platform, we built solutions and put it out there, we iterated a little with the help of external teachers like Dacher Keltner and Jon Kabat-Zinn for the consumer stuff, and Marc Brackett for bullying among teenagers. With a little bit of iteration, we were able to get really fantastic results.

Once we got it right and the measurements were fantastic, things were on a roll. We learned how important it is to work within the incentive structure, so we were honoring the environment we were in.

Measurement is critical. The interesting question in capturing customer care experiences is, is it measured in such a way that it conveys to the management the suffering of the people who are contacting you. How many people are hanging up the phone? Are they happy? And if your company facilitates connections as Facebook does, what connections go sideways, what are the negative impacts? So in our case, when people came to us with their suffering, we started asking what can we do about that. We learned from traditions, from social science, from experts and applied it at work. We built products that would fulfill needs, and kept surveying information, and tracking if we are meeting the demand, because it is important to demonstrate that we are creating a positive impact. When we build, we always see from our perspective, not necessarily what people are experiencing. When we have data, the data will speak to leadership. That is what I was able to do, with fantastic support from the management. I have yet to come across a leader, who when you present a measurement of these things, will not pay attention. Imagine that customer service metric was not necessarily to get a rating for satisfaction but about how you make people feel at the end of the conversation, including when they did not get what they wanted, and they still feel heard, respected, acknowledged. And when this happens, and the measurements happen, doors will open.

Taking a business-centric approach is critical to building human-centric programs in your organization. The important question to ask is: 'What is aligned with my company's mission and community? Is it in service of the mission of the place I am at?' And then look around and figure out where the pain that can be eased is. And then understand how it can be measured. And then there is a body of knowledge and tools out there that can guide on how we can create solutions and get along. Part of doing this is about understanding what the purpose of your company is. It is not going to be like that in every place, but there are plenty of opportunities.

If you are a person trying to create change in your company, you first need to understand how your environment operates, and the moment your heart gets lit up, and you are able to see something within the mission of your company that can be measured, and you know you can do this and be of service. Sometimes people who orient with the work forget that others need to see measurements. For example, if you are building compassion in your workplace, you could work with HR and look at health surveys, and find if there are there questions in those surveys that measure the levels of suffering, anxiety, stress? You put together the data and take it to management and management will want to do something about it. And as they look for solutions, you will be able to offer compassion as the solution. We began this journey, and it opened doors to create suicide prevention programs, among the best of its kind. We created guides for parents to talk to their teenagers when they are being bullied. When done the right way, companies really can become a force of good in their communities. **"**

Governments and Compassion

So far, we have considered how compassion can be implemented at the level of organizations. Let's expand on the thinking and discuss how we can expand compassion culture beyond organizations. Let's think scale- let's think governments. Governments can and should be the drivers of compassion cultures. This is not to infringe on personal choices or beliefs of individuals, but to provide a context for how their population shows up on the global stage. This is the foundation of a country's peace and prosperity, and like organizations, establishes a certain attractiveness for the rest of the world.

"Love and compassion are necessities, not luxuries. Without them, humanity cannot survive."
— **His Holiness the Dalai Lama, The Art of Happiness**

Material wealth is currently the single largest denominator of success and power in societies. Obsessive materialism is in part responsible for most of the global issues and sustainability challenges the world is facing. There is a fear of losing out in the global race for physical wealth. The question is, which countries will be the first to challenge the paradigm and shift the definition of success from greed to compassion. Compassionate societies are naturally happy societies. A compassionate society, by focusing on the alleviation of suffering for all of its members, nurtures equity, justice, fairness, tolerance, accountability, access to resources and quality of life, ecological sustainability, as well as harmony with other societies and communities around them. Compassionate societies de-emphasize greed and resist values based on financial hierarchy.

It takes a lot of courage and faith to edge away from the global definitions of success based on financial wealth, but it can be done. The country of Bhutan is a leader in this space.

Bhutan has chosen to use the philosophy of **Gross National Happiness** (GNH) to define its governance. GNH is an index to measure the collective happiness and well-being of a population. The king of Bhutan adopted GNH in the 1970s with the idea that all human beings strive for happiness and a country's development should be measured by its citizens' happiness. The GNH Center at Bhutan, which oversees the implementation of GNH, defines this as "a holistic and sustainable approach to development, which balances material and non-material values with the conviction that humans want to search for happiness. The objective of GNH is to achieve a balanced development in all the facets of life that are essential; for our happiness."[3]

What this means is that Bhutan includes non-material goals of happiness and sustainability in all of its policies. GNH is built on four pillars: Sustainable and Equitable Socio-economic development, Good governance, Environmental conservation and preservation, and Promotion of culture. Under these broad four domains, GNH seeks to address the wellbeing of multiple domains of living that includes psychological wellbeing, health, education, living standards, cultural resilience, time use, good governance, community vitality, and environment.

The economic health of a country is critical for the happiness of its citizens. The comprehensive definition of GNH, which includes the economic development of its citizens, creates a balanced approach to grow as a country while still focusing on happiness. So much so that, in 2011, The UN General Assembly passed Resolution "Happiness: towards a holistic approach to development" urging member nations to follow the example of Bhutan and measure happiness and well-being and calling happiness a "fundamental human goal."[4]

Our current global economic policies are a juggernaut racing toward an unsustainable future for our children, and the world is starting to wake up to this reality. Global communities can tap into Bhutan's experiments with GNH to learn and be inspired by.

Another country that has chartered a vision toward happiness is the United Arab Emirates, which ranks highest in levels of happiness in the Middle East, according to the World Happiness Report. The United Arab Emirates has even appointed a Minister of State for Happiness and launched the National Programme for Happiness and Positivity[5]. They released a guide to happiness and well-being in the workplace with a stated purpose 'to help government entities and other stakeholders in the private sector and non-profit organizations discover how to foster the conditions necessary for employees to thrive and flourish at work in terms of productivity and engagement.'

United Arab Emirate's National program for happiness and positivity covers three areas:
> inclusion of happiness in the policies, programs and services of all government bodies and at work;
> promotion of positivity and happiness as a lifestyle in the community;
> and development of benchmarks and tools to measure happiness.'

As part of its happiness initiative, UAE's happiness program plans to appoint personnel trained in areas including the science of happiness and positivity, mindfulness, leading a happy team, happiness and policies in government work, measuring happiness. Even though the program is in its early days, the intent and effort of the UAE to foster happiness are inspiring.

Speaking of happiness as a measure, the United Nations presents a yearly ranking of countries based on perceived happiness. The ranking primarily takes into account these six factors: income, healthy life expectancy, social support, freedom, trust, and generosity. The Scandinavian countries of Denmark, Switzerland, Norway, and Finland have consistently featured as the happiest countries in the world in the past several years[6] While the emphasized terminology is 'happiness', I believe the underlying narrative here is compassion. Compassion, I believe, is the most effective social framework (the means) to create the outcome of long-term happiness(the end).

New Zealand's young Prime Minister, Ms. Jacinda Ardern, while addressing the general debate of the 73rd Session of the General Assembly of the UN, set a bold vision for her country founded on kindness, empathy, and inclusion. To this effect, starting in 2019, her government has presented a "well-being budget", the first of its kind in the world, budget tackling mental illness, family violence and child poverty[7].

But the world's largest governments are yet to commit to shift toward a culture of compassion. Many leaders choose to ignore the bigger picture of a collective, thriving humanity in favor of narrow, divisive policies guised as patriotism. It will take a radical shift in our mindsets. *We will have to look beyond narrow walls of divisive politics and create a vision for a future of inclusive abundance.* I believe this starts with compassion skilling the decision-makers. Compassion skilling, offered as training programs, not only equips political leaders with the tools, but also gives the mental freedom to make pro-compassionate choices for the people they lead. Once they understand that compassion is not a disadvantage, but a platform that gives them the populist advantage, more and more politicians will be convinced to practice and promote compassion in their governance. Besides, doing the right thing creates a worthy legacy, which is the aspiration of political office.

Below are some of the ideas for political leaders to create and nurture a future of compassion in their countries. It is important to acknowledge at the outset that this is a slow, deliberate process and fraught with extraordinary challenges that come from swimming against established opinion. But I do believe that there is no better time for this change than now.

Skilling and Tooling political leaders in compassionate governance

A great place to start is by training political leadership in the tenets of compassion. A good compassion-training program should create a clear vision of what is possible, advocate the feasibility of the compassion framework, provide the skills and tools to implement compassionate change in their communities, offer them ways to measure the successes and failures of their efforts. Many of the tools outlined in the book can be adopted for training compassionate governance.

Education

It is time to move towards a kinder, less competitive curriculum. The models and scope of education are continually shifting. What remains constant though, is that educational systems as we see them today are focused on knowledge accumulation. Two decades ago, knowledge was the key success differentiator. Today, in the age of the internet, knowledge has become superfluous. The age of the solo-genius is behind us. The most successful people in general tend to be those who have the skills to influence and lead others, have the emotional capacity for resilience, and who can creatively harness a collective vision. These are skills of emotional intelligence, which people are expected to gather as they go through life.

A smarter educational system, which aims to future skill its people, will adapt its schooling to include the development of emotional intelligence skills from the outset. Compassion, like all good skills, can be learned and accessed readily with practice. Compassion training as essential part of the educational model will bring down our crime rates, create prosperity, develop governance that will emphasize conservation and sustainability, and support a global culture of happiness. *Using compassion training as a curriculum from a very early stage of schooling can avoid many of the current systemic challenges in schools, including bullying, suicides, and school shootings that are becoming increasingly common.* When young minds learn to notice their suffering and feel safe to address it in a safe space, we could end up seeing a different set of conversations among students and eventually in the world they will create. It is heartening to see schools adopting mindfulness practices as an alternative to punishment.

Singapore has set a new tone for non-competitive education by abolishing school exam rankings. Finland, which has among the best educational systems in the world, emphasizes social skills education even at preschool levels, easy access to quality teachers, and opportunities for higher education.

When countries forget to demonstrate the value for their teachers, entire educational systems can be shaken. As educators are expected to demonstrate compassion to the children they nurture, it follows that educators should be given the compassionate support and trainings that they are expected to disseminate. Educational systems should also try to include opportunities to actively explore other cultures and perspectives without bias. Cultural sensitivity and inclusion training does not have to wait until individuals enter office settings.

Here is a story of how one school has successfully experimented with a schooling system based on kindness and compassion. **Andy Smallman** founded the **Puget Sound Community School (PSCS)** in Seattle in 1994 with a vision to change the way students experience life during their most impactful years.

"The primary thing children do at most schools, their primary source of motivation, is to get through the day avoiding humiliation. Humiliation can take many forms. From taunts on the school bus, in the classroom, or on the playground, to what they wear or bring for lunch, to whether or not a teacher will call on them in class and they will not know the answer, students are working hard to save face. Schools and teachers need to understand that students in this mindset are not in the best position to learn anything but how to survive their schooling experience. Their brains are not able to absorb new and potentially meaningful information.

To offset this, schools need to first focus on creating environments in which students feel safe and supported for being themselves. Schools need structures to acknowledge and celebrate diversity in all forms, so students experience the joy that comes from being unique. In such settings, teachers become facilitators, mentors, and guides who help young people identify and step outside of their comfort zones, to stretch and grow, just like they comfortably did when they were babies and toddlers.

In 1993, I proposed what in 1994 became the Puget Sound Community School, a progressive middle and high school in Seattle founded on the premise that provided a loving and nurturing school environment and no mandatory academic classes or standardized tests, young people will learn everything they need to lead happy, productive lives. At PSCS, the way young people learn is to be immersed in a collaborative educational community that respects and honors their individuality, challenges them to step outside their comfort zones, and encourages them to pursue those things that bring them joy. So honored, PSCS students discover and learn to use their natural gifts. In the process, they develop a deep sense of self and create meaningful expressions of their passions in the world.

Learning at PSCS is defined as an activity of life, not just preparation for it. The school's emphasis is on how to think, not what to think. Students work each year with an advisor to identify their short and long-term goals, and plan for what they want to accomplish and how, both individually and collaboratively, regardless of their age. Learning takes place in different settings according to scheduled and spontaneous classes and activities facilitated by members of the teaching staff, trained volunteers, and even occasionally by fellow students. Activity offerings change regularly and are driven not only by what students need to help them achieve their goals, but also by their thirst to investigate new themes or topics.

Now that's all well and good, but the "secret sauce" behind the success at PSCS is the school being grounded in kindness, compassion, and gratitude. Each day begins in a school-wide meeting called "check-in." Facilitated by one of the students who makes the decision to take the leadership role without coercion, check-in lasts no more than 15 minutes and includes time for people to make announcements, to identify two students who volunteer to ready the kitchen for school use, and, most importantly, time for any member of the school to share an "appreciation." In sum, an appreciation is a very short story of gratitude that an individual wants an audience to hear. It can be for a parent, a random event, or for another member of the school community. Really, it can be about anything. The critical thing is that is it something positive.

This part of check-in is often the longest, and it's not uncommon for appreciations to include stories about bus drivers singing out the stops, a parent taking extra time to make a child's favorite breakfast, or for seeing the sunrise. In fact, the significance of appreciations at PSCS is so big that an afternoon meeting, check-out, was initiated so the school day would end on the same positive note that it began.

Of perhaps even greater significance, the school's graduation ceremony evolved years ago to become centered on appreciating the graduating seniors. Each June, each of the school's graduating students is held in appreciation by the community for 30 minutes. During this time, looked forward to for years by the students and their parents, stories are told about the seniors and reminisces are shared. It's not uncommon for a younger student to share how a graduating student had positively impacted them, nor is it uncommon for alumni to return in order to appreciate students with whom they had interacted. To say that tears are shed is an understatement; in fact, one parent once commented that if the PSCS graduation ceremony could be bottled and shared throughout the world, we'd have peace on Earth.

The 21st century has brought a new era of innovation and access to information. Successful people have developed critical thinking skills to assimilate, analyze, and draw meaningful conclusions from vast and disparate sources of information, and know-how to effectively communicate and collaborate to address real-world needs. Unfortunately, mainstream education has not kept up with the times. PSCS is a conscious attempt to provide an educational experience for young people that best positions them for success in the world in which we now live. PSCS maintains a school community that appreciates people for who they are right now. This humanistic approach allows students to experience personal success and fulfillment in the present and the future as capable, engaged adults.

Over the school's 25 years, I've often been asked what students do after having graduated from PSCS. The question generally is being asked with sincere curiosity, but I sometimes recognize it as skepticism in disguise, as if young people raised in such an educational environment won't be prepared to deal with the harshness of the so-called "real world." The simplest way to respond is to say that PSCS graduates go on to do things just like 18 year-olds from other high schools. They go to college, and they travel, they take a gap year before making a commitment. What I've found is that whatever they choose to do, they make the decision mindfully. When it comes to college, they tend to choose smaller colleges that provide them a more intimate setting. And they all find themselves well-prepared, especially so for having made so many important educational decisions as high school students. In fact, they often report how immature they find other freshmen. I'm proud to say that the school's graduates include teachers, counselors, software engineers, tattoo artists, and clothing designers. I'm prouder to say that PSCS graduates embody the school's vision to send out into the world global ambassadors for a philosophy that values kindness, wholeness, and social justice. **"**

Media

Media has the power to shift how compassion is viewed by the populace. Our individual biases and our collective consciousness is driven by traditional and social media. What we define as right and wrong can be easily shifted by deluges of media information. In that sense, our identities are merely puppets to a media-driven frenzy. That is not to demonize media. Media is merely a dispersed function of people catering to the information needs of the populace. And the populace demands sensationalism. That is why a beautiful story about human kindness is displaced by an atrocious (but certainly more 'juicy' report) about a school shooter. With one feeding into the other, media and collective consciousness seems on a no-return path of negative sensationalism.

Some media outlets have taken the effort to include inspirational stories of kindness as part of their mainstream offering, but media also has to practice restraint in drumming up energy around negative news. Media can create urgency around the need for compassion. I think the time is ripe to create sensationalism around compassion. Some of it can be achieved by making compassion training as part of journalistic ethics. A conscious choice must be made by journalists to return the ethics of unbiased news for news sake, with a clear understanding of their role in creating a compassionate society.

Due recognition

There is an unspoken belief that anything that is based on human kindness and service must not have a reward or recognition attached to it. While compassion is a natural spontaneous response to suffering, the bias that giving without expectation should never be rewarded is dis-compassionate. This follows the same line of thought that nonprofits must offer their services for free and that non-profit business owners should not experience comfort, because they are morally obliged to be altruistic. It is okay to be rewarded for being kind. It is okay to offer compassion in broad daylight and be acknowledged for it. It is okay to allow ourselves to be appreciated and valued for the compassion we bring to the world without expectations. As we discussed in the Self-compassion chapter, receiving is just as much an expression of compassion as giving. Programs like CNN Heroes recognize the extraordinary contribution of individuals in the space of compassion. Programs like these must become more common. After all, compassion needs to be celebrated too!

Punishment systems

This is a story about a tribe in South Africa which has a very unique way of dealing with crime and punishment. When a member of the tribe is proven guilty of crime, all work in the village comes to a halt. The villagers set the transgressor in the middle of the village. Instead of punishment, the villagers start hurling kindness toward that person. They recollect every good thing they can think of about the transgressor and thank him/her for that. This goes on until all good things about the person have been said. Finally, the transgressor expresses regret for his/her actions. Then the village holds a feast, as a symbolic 'welcome-back' for the transgressor into their community. It is said that crimes in this tribe are almost non-existent.

This approach seems almost antithetical to the idea of punishment, but I believe the story contrasts and challenges the current perception of crime and punishment in most other countries, including the USA. But a few countries are experimenting with compassionate punishments, keeping the goal in mind that jail time is meant to reform, not punish, and the ultimate goal is to create a safer, kinder society. Norway, for example, has minimum security prisons called *Bastøy,* which are designed to feel like college dorms. Each prisoner has his own room with TV, computers, heated floors, community rooms. Some Bastoys even feature a full recording studio. The idea of Bastoy is to take away the freedom of transgressors, but still treat them with dignity and humanity. This lenient approach has actually helped reduce Norway's crime rates. Keeping the compassion in dealing with crime, in policing, judicial processes, and incarceration- creating responses to crime that are appropriately tough but still human- will go a long way in reducing the levels of repeat offenses. The ultimate goal should be to heal and reintegrate rather than hurt and isolate.

Another compassionate policy in dealing with crime is to stop de-humanizing the formerly incarcerated, and giving them the possibility to re-enter society with grace and work-opportunities. Policies that help treat people with compassion in the entire process of dealing with crime can help not only the happiness levels of coun-

tries, but also reduce crime, save resources, and improve econo-
mies.

Fairness and equity in resource distribution

Compassion is only a fancy word when a society's reality is that of
hardship and poverty. A close up view of many high GDP countries shows that wealth is localized to a small segment of the populace. When resources are not equitably distributed, and when there
is a looming sense of inequality in society, there is a natural lack of
compassion and happiness.

Environmental sustainability

Without a sustainable world to live in, all discussions on compassion are meaningless. Our planet is suffering, and we are beginning
to feel it too. Unlike the dinosaurs who had no control over their
extinction, we have the capacity to alter our future to some level.
As we think of compassion for our workplaces and the people
around us, I also want to call you to think of compassion for our
ailing planet. Preserving and protecting our little spaceship with
compassion is essential if humanity to exist.

Nnaumrata Arora Singh
India Lead, Charter for Compassion and Founder, Zhemyna
Foundation

"**P**ope Francis offers to us that 'Rather than a problem to
be solved, the world is a joyful mystery to be contemplated with
gladness and praise'.

It is tough to think of the world like that in the light of Climate Change - the dreaded ghost in the daunting castle of the An-
thropocene. It haunts our humanity as we slowly tread towards
what is now being referred to as the Sixth Extinction. Climate activists, environmentalists, change-makers all over the world are
feeling overwhelmed and weighed down with the magnitude of the
problem we have at hand.

The truth that is being unveiled in uncomfortable pieces, thanks to social media and some courageous organizations, is enabling us to realize how the slow poison of consumerism has been fed to us over time by virtue of carefully crafted messaging. We have been made to believe by large corporations that we are not ok, that something is wrong with us and the only way we can be ok is for us to buy 'something'. That something is what they sell and we buy. We buy into their story of our inadequacy. That then, becomes the driving force for this economy that we all are living in; an economy, that is not working for our planet.

As Wendell Berry wonderfully reminds us: 'The care of the Earth is our most ancient and most worthy, and after all, our most pleasing responsibility. To cherish what remains of it and to foster its renewal is our only legitimate hope.'

But how do we really get started given where we are? How do we deal with the polarized world that we have collectively created? On the one hand, we have the profit-driven capitalists who choose to travel even small distances by choppers and private jets, and on the other hand, we are faced with 70.8 million people who have been rendered homeless. How do we reconcile with the fact that while millions of homes are abandoned around the world, millions of people still roam around homeless? Or that one-third of the food that is produced in the world is wasted even though one in nine people in the world go hungry?

The situation today can be overwhelming for anyone, and many people have chosen to live in denial. We deny that we have a shared moral responsibility with the rest of humanity, for protecting our forests and flora and fauna. Living in denial of our shared humanity also means living a life that is disconnected with ourselves. No wonder then that there is an increase in the level of isolation faced by people around the world, across age groups, and an increase in the depression and suicide rates.

So what do we do? Not everyone is cut out to be an activist or a change maker. What is it that each of us can do, where we are?

Satish Kumar, in his essay on Soil, Soul, and Society in Spiritual Ecology, reminds us that 'Our human responsibility is to restore and maintain harmony'.

Researchers and peacebuilders around the world agree on this one thing - what we most need to do today is to find ways of bringing people together and restoring our sense of community and belongingness.

In her book Active Hope, Joanna Macy says, 'To promote the recovery of our world and the healing of our communities, while also leading lives that are rich and satisfying, we need to embody a larger story of who and what we are. She further goes on to say 'Our connected self is based on recognizing that we are a part of many larger circles'.

We can do everything in our personal capacity to reverse global warming - we can stop using plastics, start composting at home, buy less, become a minimalist, adopt a raw vegan lifestyle, buy local and organic, use solar heating and everything else that we are being told to do. However, if we are doing this in isolation and not able to engage our community or if we continue to live in a disharmonious space or if we feel hatred for the person next door, then we have basically failed at the most important task there is, for birthing our new Earth.

The solution to many problems the world is facing today might sound simplistic, but it really starts with having a compassionate conversation. By being able to give our undivided attention to the person next to us, and subsequently to many people around us, by opening our hearts to them and being able to listen to them, with our full presence, is what each of us can do. I invite each of us to start with that.

Climate change statistics, IPCC reports, the melting of ice caps, yes, all that is real, but let us put all that aside. Let us focus on what we can do, here and now. One thing perhaps that merits discussion is that, it is our disconnection with ourselves that could get in the way, and hence, the work we might end up doing for self-restoration might really be the most important work we have to do on this planet during our lifetime.

Meditation is going great guns nowadays, and practices like mindfulness certainly help, but the one thing which I have found to be most successful in helping us heal our broken parts and joyfully so, is the simple act of service. Can we make time to be of service to those around us, without expectations, without an agenda and without any end objective in mind? Can we just be present and listen? Listening to another being is perhaps the biggest form of service we can offer to humankind today. It is through this simple act of fostering connection that we can hope for our hearts to transform, and from that chrysalis, we will see our new Earth emerge. **"**

The Fifth Revolution: Working toward a compassionate future

We are approaching a humanity which will increasingly depend on technology and artificial intelligence (AI) for handling everyday needs. Our job profiles are changing. Kai Fu Lee, a pioneer of AI and the founder of Sinovation Ventures, China, estimates that AI will replace 40% of human jobs will be replaced in the next 15 years by AI[8]. But it will also create new job functions, and perhaps even new industries. Workplaces might become increasingly virtual and the nature of workplace relationships could be dramatically different from what they are now. Job functions may likely be split between humans and machines, with human functions becoming more and more machine interfacing.

Still, innovation and creativity will remain in the human domain, and human relationships in workplaces are still going to drive innovation, creativity, and business success. In whatever ways our jobs evolve, as long as there is a need for human relationships regarding work, our needs for happiness, to feel valued and empowered will remain. My belief is that compassion will continue to give the success edge for businesses by empowering people in whatever roles they take on. When we are skilling our workplaces with compassion, we are upskilling for our future success. **The call of the Fifth revolution is to make a conscious choice for a future where we, as humans, still get our due nourishment of mind** and spirit through compassion, however the profile of jobs or the future of work turns out to be.

The revolution of compassion also assures us that we need not approach the dynamism of technology with fear or angst, since we will have the umbrella skills to handle what changes may come, with grace.

Daniel Doulton, CPO, Sceye, offers this perspective on how **compassion still matters in a world of AI.**

"What makes a machine different from humans?

Artificial intelligence (AI) - software that can self-learn to create 'humanized' intelligence - is one of humanity's most ambitious undertakings. It is also potentially an undertaking that could redefine humanity as it exists today. As Tesla founder Elon Musk stated, "AI is far more dangerous than nukes," (SXSW meeting) while Stephen Hawking believed that, "the development of full artificial intelligence could spell the end of the human race".

Intelligence, in general, is difficult to define. So therefore is AI. Experts in the AI space describe three types of AI:

1. Artificial Narrow Intelligence (ANI): using massive computing power to master routine challenges through iterative learning.

2. Artificial General Intelligence (AGI): when human-level thinking becomes possible, including the abstract, creative, multi-angle thinking that the human brain is capable of.

3. Artificial Super Intelligence (ASI): when AI has reached AGI levels and enormous computing power allows AI to master every field and aspect of collective humanity.

Historically, we are in the early days of AI. Our greatest progress has been with Narrow AI. Consider the example of AlphaGo Zero, which mastered thousands of years of Go strategy in just a few weeks, without any human intervention, and overnight became the greatest Go player on Earth today. Or consider self-driving cars whose technology is constantly learning from daily street runs. Or voice recognition software that is learning from the extensive data that it collects from its human interactions and constantly improving its accuracy and comprehension.

However, narrow AI is focused on single, routine tasks, and does not present the kind of threat to our species that AI is often reckoned to be. But with the vast computing power of computers, narrow AI will replace many routine human jobs over time.

AI (and machine learning) is being heralded as the 4th Industrial Revolution, or the 2nd Machine Age (IT and Computational after Power and Mechanical) and as ever, there are a wide range of predictions about where it is leading. Opinions range from AI signaling a dystopian end to humans to a far more utopian existence, where machines take away the demeaning tasks nobody really wants to perform, liberating humanity to pursue what it does best.

But before we get ahead of ourselves, we must first understand the sources of cause and effect.

It is debatable whether we will achieve AGI, let alone ASI, but even if we do, we must remember that AI is simply a highly reduced synthesis of how the human brain works. And where it is lacking, we've seemingly made up by applying huge computational power to boost its performance, a brute force technique, not intelligence. So it is unlikely to achieve consciousness and gain self-generated intention. Humans are designing and setting its parameters or tasks and objectives, and while AI may exhibit human-like efficiency and seemingly creative ways to achieve the objective, it nonetheless only exists for that objective, one a human set.

AI brings up one of human's biggest existential questions: *what is consciousness, and can it be fabricated, or it is created from a higher-order realm? And really, can something create something larger than itself, namely, could we create intelligence beyond our own? Can we be Gods, or are we incapable of breaking our subjugation?*

AI embodies a very human need to personify inanimate objects so that we can relate to them and give them a more human role, much as we do with our pets, or even virtual pets such as Tamagotchi. And paradoxically, we fall in the trap of assuming it has a conscience and intent, and we give it power over us.

The head spins. The centuries pass. We're still here.

So, I'd suggest we put our hubris aside and take stock of facts: we haven't yet exceeded ourselves, and we don't have anything other than our fantasy of doing so, so it is surely still out of our reach.

Regardless, what is really important is the intent that we put into what we create. To date, we've created amazing technologies that have truly freed us up and allowed us to prosper economically. The difference with AI is that, whilst it takes away cognitive tasks, it is a technology that replaces one of the distinct features that makes us human, namely our ability to perform cognitive tasks. And the more AI replaces specific cognitive tasks, and does them better than humans, the more threatened we feel, the less valued we feel. We don't know where we fit and what we'll become next. We are social creatures and need purpose, connection, and we often attach much of this to our work, our function, which is why AI, whilst improving our work/life is actually challenging our sense of purpose. And because of this, AI does pose a real risk to our psyche, our collective sense of being and society's well-being.

Perhaps it takes an existential crisis for humans to dig in and bring out the best of our humanity; when we realize that we actively need to nurture and protect human worth and values, not trade it unwittingly for a short-term economic gain.

And this is where the real work of compassion comes to help us design technology with respect. With awareness of the painful displacements that AI may bring, and the need to put our values first, that humans are more important than the economic value of any machine and that we must balance commercial gain with social enrichment. No other outcome is worthy.

The natural risk is that AI may be designed without this context and so create unintended pain as a by-product, or it is used by a bad actor where the intention is myopic or maligned.

There is no doubt that AI will come, proliferate and replace many cognitive tasks we all do (yes, all of us, even CEO's reading this) and we are facing an existential crisis. This is why we should consciously choose how we design AI in a cultural context as much as in a functional or economic context.

It is strange that as an entrepreneurial spirit, I would advocate controls and governance, but I do so to ensure we all give ourselves a prod and realise that our greatest human skills are in great need. We need to muster our higher-order qualitative thinking as to how best to balance these benefits with human values and engineer our way successfully out of our own existential crisis.

By doing so, we will connect with a vision of our positive future and work towards that as our intent, rather than allowing this technology to bump its way through society and risk causing psychological and societal damage.

So what does this mean in practical terms?

AI needs to serve humans and meet our rational needs. Here are some examples:

- AI should self-identify to humans that it is AI. Otherwise, it creates ambiguity and distrust, so it needs to be respectful that it is serving a human, not equalling or tricking it. This is key for AI and a risk to its existence.
- AI should explain its objective, goals or purpose
- AI should explain what it will do next if asked
- AI should explain why it did (will do) something so humans can understand its workings and predict its behavior
- AI should always place a human's safety above its own
- AI should always obey a human's command, except when this is to threaten or harm another - in other words seek to always behave safely AI's benefits need to be balanced with human values
- The value (or savings) created by AI needs to be balanced with the loss of that human's role
- The introduction of AI needs to be done in collaboration with the humans that it affects
- We need smart humans to design a good framework for how to think about and plan AI's introduction in a human-values centered way
- We need an industry or independent body to help develop basic standards of positive AI that AI providers can certify to and display their badge showing they use/conform and support 'positive AI'.

Consciously working to use AI in a human-centred way, we will develop a far wider awareness and capability in society to better manage ourselves, how we treat each other and learn that by putting compassion at the heart of what we do, we will have created sustainable value for us all, not just a few, and grown as a society. **"**

How can I become a force of compassion in my community and my country? What are three tangible actions I can commit to to be a compassion ambassador in my society?

_____

_____

_____

_____

_____

_____

_____

_____

_____

_____

_____

_____

_____

_____

Conclusion

This is it, Folks!

Thank you for taking this journey with me!

We started our book exploring compassion skills to use as individuals, as influencers, and as leaders. We discussed how we can use compassion frameworks to shift work cultures and governments. We reflected, experimented on ourselves and our workplaces, created strategies for lifelong changes. We are in a good place. Now it is time to pass on the goodness. I hope you will become an evangelist of compassion in your world, in whatever way you see fit.

We as human beings have to walk a narrow road between being consumers and being givers. We cannot deny our financial or social realities. But, at the end of the day, if we end up leaving more goodness than we took, we would have walked a compassionate path.

Just as a reminder: Look back to the Self-Reflection exercise on page at the beginning of the book where you listed your top 5 current challenges. After you have had a chance to experiment with compassion skills, work on the second column of this exercise. See how your perception of those challenges have shifted.

As you step out on your compassion journey...

I hope you found more than information in this book.

I hope you found inspiration that can fundamentally shift the way you see and embrace your world.

I hope as you go about your life after reading this book, and when life throws its curveballs at you, you will remember that you have a choice to react with compassion.

I also hope you remember that should you choose to react with compassion, all the skills and tools are available for you.

As you make more and more of compassion choices, I hope it becomes easier and easier to practice compassion. I hope compassion becomes your way of being in your workplace and outside and that you become the beacon that others look up to for their own inspiration.

May you be free from danger and anxiety. May you be loved. May you find happiness every step of the way.

Much love

Dr. Immanual Joseph, Ph.D. , CPC

Contributors

My special thanks to the contributors

	Name	Designation
1	Dr. James Doty	Stanford Neurosurgeon, Founder of CCARE Stanford
2	Amuthan Sundar	Senior Business Analyst
3	Daniel Doulton	CPO, Sceye
4	Birju Pandya	Social Impact Investor
5	Santalynda Marrero	Coach, Diversity Consultant
6	Mandar Apte	Former Shell Manager, Founder 'From India with Love'
7	Dani Savekar	CEO GLAS group
8	Ferose VR	Senior Vice President, SAP Labs Silicon Valley
9	Dan Waldschmidt	Founder of EDGY, Author and Keynote speaker
10	Lindsay Benjamin	Mindfulness Lead, Shell
11	Loretta Breuning	Founder, Inner Mammalian Institute
12	Nishita Bharadwaj	IT Delivery Manager VMWare
13	Chandra Elango	Head of IT, Go To Market, Atlassian
14	Melissa Sutor	Mindfulness teacher
15	Shelley Winner	Surface Specialist, Microsoft
16	Grant Nowell	IT Operations Manager, VMWare

17	Joe Hansen	Transformational Change consultant, Shell
18	Karen Palmer	Founder, GlobalKindness going Viral
19	Rachel Weissman	Interaction Designer, Google
20	Adam Burn	Program Analyst, US Department of Veterans Affairs
21	Nnaumrata Arora	India Lead, Charter for Compassion and Founder, Zhemyna Foundation
22	Andy Smallman	Founder, Puget Sound Community School
23	Arturo Bejar	Former Head of Engineering, Facebook
24	Trish Stevens	Founder, Ascot Media
25	Ramanathan Meyyappan	Senior Manager, VMWare
26	Narayanan Krishnan	Founder, Akshaya Trust
27	Kristin Gordon	Assistant professor of Sociology at GeorgiaTech

And others who shared their stories and perspectives but chose to stay anonymous.

Thank you!

I am indebted to the incredible humans in my life who have believed in my compassion journey and been my great pillars of support.

Here is a partial list:

My family-Savitha Sundar, my wife and best friend. My children Iniyan and Nila, who inspire me more than any book ever could. My siblings Gerry, Aloysius and Kamala. And my mother, Mary Litween, who modeled compassion through her life, and taught me the power of stories.

My amazing mentors- Rajesh Setty, Karl Mehta, Dr. James Doty.

My compassion partners and friends- Komal Kanal, Amuthan Sundar, Karen Palmer, Nnumrata Arora, Rakhee, Ram Meyappan, Varuna, RJ Sudha, Deepak Goel, Wendi Gilbert, Madhu Sudha, Ning Go, TJ, Dioni Ha...and the list goes on!

Would you like to add your story to the collective wisdom? Please visit https://www.fifthrevolution.life/your-stories

References

Introduction

1. Case Study: Karoshi: Death from overwork.   23 April 2013. International Labor Organization. ilo.org.
2. Karõshi. Wikipedia. en.wikipedia.org.
3. Nurfriti Moeslim, Jan 13, 2018. iNSAMER.

Section 1: Compassion

1. University study by Michael Solomon, Ph.D., Marketing Department Graduate School of Business, NYU
2. Empathy and compassion, Tania Singer and Olga Klimecki. Current Biology 2014. Vol 24, Issue 18, Pgs R875 - R878.
3. Visual Attention to Suffering After Compassion Training is Associated With Decreased Amygdala Responses. Helen Y. Weng et al. 2018. Front Psychol. 9: 771.
4. Vagus Nerve. Wikipedia. https://en.wikipedia.org.
5. A role of central oxytocin in autonomic functions: its action in the motor nucleus of the vagus nerve. Dreifuss JJ et al. 1988. Brain Res Bull. Jun; 20(6): 765-70.
6. Relations of School Children's Comforting Behavior to Empathy-Related Reactions and Shyness. Nancy Eisenberg et al. 2006. Social Development 5(3): 330-351.
7. The inflammatory reflex. Kevin J. Tracey. 2002. Nature Vol 420. 19/26.
8. Upward spirals of the heart: autonomic flexibility, as indexed by vagal tone, reciprocally and prospectively predicts positive emotions and social connectedness. Biol Psychol. 2010 Dec;85(3):432-6.

9. Affective and physiological responses to the suffering of others: compassion and vagal activity. J Pers Soc Psychol. 2015 Apr;108(4):572-85.

10. The Vagus Nerve at the Interface of the Microbiota-Gut-Brian Axis. Bruno Bonaz et al. 2018. Front Neurosci. 12: 49

11. Maslow, A.H. (1943)11. "A theory of human motivation." Psychological Review. 50 (4): 370–96.

12. American Time Use Survey Summary. Bureau of Labor Statistics. June 19, 2019. USDL-19-1003

13. Lottery Winners and Accident Victims: Is Happiness Relative? Philip Brickman and Dan Coates. Journal of Personality and Social Psychology. 1978, Vol. 36, No. 8, 917-927

14. Gallup's State of the American Workplace: 2010-2012 report.

15. Should I stay or should I go?. Haiya Zhang et al., IBM Smarter Workforce Institute, Thought Leadership Whitepaper. July 2017.

16. Turning around employee turnover. Jennifer Robison. Gallup News. May 8, 2008.

17. 2013 Work Stress Survey. Everest College.

18. It really pays to have a rich company culture. Eric Siu. Entrepreneur. October 2014.

19. The Most Empathetic Companies, 2016. Belinda Parmar. Harvard Business Review. December 2016.

20. What's better, money or a nice boss? NBC survey shows what we really think. Joan Raymond. Today.com. 2015

21. Happiness and productivity: Understanding the happy-productive worker. Daniel Sgroi. Social Market Foundation. October 2015.

22. The social economy: Unlocking value and productivity through social technologies. July 2012. McKinsey & Company

Section 2: The 9-Pillars of Workplace Compassion

1. Dr. Kristin Neff. Self-compassion.org
2. Neff KD. Self-compassion. The proven power of being kind to yourself. New York: Harper Collins publisher; 2015.
3. The Power of Forgiveness - Gary Ridgway. Youtube.com. https://www.youtube.com/watch?v=f2_OOaP763k
4. What Google learned from its quest to build the perfect team. Charles Duhigg. Feb 2015. The New York Times Magazine.
5. Psychological Safety and Learning Behavior in Work Teams. Amy Edmondson. Administrative Science Quarterly, Vol. 44, No. 2 (Jun., 1999), pp. 350-383
6. Google Spent 2 Years Studying 180 Teams. The Most Successful Ones Shared These 5 Traits. Michael Schneider. July 19, 2017.
7. Why Is Psychological Safety so Important in Health Care? Youtube.com. Amy Edmondson. https://www.youtube.com/watch?v=LF1253YhEc8
8. Moral behavior in animals | Frans de Waal. Youtube.com. https://www.youtube.com/watch?v=GcJxRqTs5nk
9. On Jonas Salk's 100th birthday, a celebration of his polio vaccine. Michael Hiltzik. Oct 28, 2014. Los Angeles Times.
10. Affective and cognitive prefrontal cortex projections to the lateral habenula in humans. Karin Vadovičová. Front Hum Neurosci. 2014; 8: 819.
11. Video: Breathing Exercises: 4-7-8 Breath. Drweil.com.
12. Open Hearts Build Lives: Positive Emotions, Induced Through Loving-Kindness Meditation, Build Consequential Personal Resources. Barbara Fredrickson et al. J Pers Soc Psychol. 2008 Nov; 95(5): 1045–1062.
13. A Wandering Mind Is an Unhappy Mind. M.A. Killingsworth and D. Gilbert. Science 12 Nov 2010: Vol. 330, Issue 6006, pp. 932
14. American Mindfulness Research Association. https://goamra.org/resources/

15. The Wood Wide Web. Anna Rothschild. February 2017. Pbs.org.
16. TV 2 | All That We Share. Youtube.com. https://www.youtube.com/watch?v=jD8tjhVO1Tc&t=26s
17. Social relationships and mortality risk: a meta-analytic review. PLoS Medicine. Holt-Lunstad J, TB, Layton JB. 2010.
18. Nazi Language and Terminology. United States Holocaust Memorial Museum. Ushmm.org.
19. The Odds Of You Being Alive Are Incredibly Small. Dina Spector. June 2012. Businessinsider.com.
20. Employee trust and workplace performance. Sarah Brown et al. Journal of Economic Behavior & Organization. Volume 116, August 2015, Pages 361-378
21. Building trust 2013: Workforce Trends Defining High Performance. June 2013. Interaction Associates.
22. The neural basis of altruistic punishment. de Quervain, D et al. 2004. Science 305,1254–1258.
23. The anterior cingulate cortex: an integrative hub for human socially-driven interactions. Claudio Lavin et al. Front Neurosci. 2013; 7: 64.

Section 3: Compassion Experiments

1. Can You Rewire Your Brain? 5 Scientific Ways To Change Emotional Habits. JR Thorpe. June 2016. Bustle.com.
2. Zeigarnik effect. Wikipedia. en.wikipedia.org.
3. Three Signs Your Company May Have a Culture Problem. Denise Pirrotti Hummel. May 16, 2019. Linkedin.

Section 4: A Systems Approach to Compassion

1. Global Human Capital Trends 2016. Deloitte Press.
2. Moai—This Tradition is Why Okinawan People Live Longer, Better. Bluezones.com
3. What is GNH? Gnhcentrebhutan.org
4. Gross National Happiness. en.wikipedia.org

5. A Guide to Happiness and Well-being at workplace. Government.ae.
6. World Happiness Report 2018.
7. New Zealand 'wellbeing' budget promises billions to care for most vulnerable. Eleanor Ainge Roy. theguardian.com.
8. Artificial intelligence will replace half of all jobs in the next decade, says widely followed technologist. Sophia Yan. Apr 2017. cnbc.com.